Footprints of a Pioneer

The Story of Yvonne

By Leola Caya Meagher

Copyright Leola Caya Meagher
First North American Rights
2996 Bay Road,
L'Orignal, ON
613-675-2996

Library and Archives Canada Cataloguing in Publication

Meagher, Leola Caya, author
     Footprints of a pioneer : the story of Yvonne / Leola
Caya Meagher.

ISBN 978-0-9952882-0-1 (paperback)

   1. Caya, Yvonne. 2. Women pioneers--Québec (Province)--
Laurentians--Biography. 3. Laurentians (Québec)--Biogra-
phy.
4. Mountain life--Québec (Province)--Laurentians. 5.
Housewives--
Québec (Province)--Laurentians. I. Title.

FC2945.L387Z49 2016   971.4'2403092
C2016-906187-6

Book layout and design by The Review,
Vankleek Hill, Ontario.

Printed by lulu.com

October 2016

I dedicate this book to my children and grandchildren
that they might know their grandmother
and great-grandmother for the special lady she was.

I trust this will inspire you to live a life
that would honour her memory.

Table of Contents

Introduction

What triggered the idea of writing a book? Before Mama died, she showed me a collection of old newspaper clippings and yellowed snapshots from the early years. These brought back a surge of memories, and as the old trunk yielded its secrets, an intriguing notion began noodling around in my mind, something bordering on insanity, perhaps. As memories scurried in to tap me on the shoulder, I entertained the thought of piecing together these remnants of the past into a quilt, and stitching it with heartstrings to warm the soul. I was walking into a giant attic full of the scraps of my past, a jumble of memorabilia, which needed to be sorted and displayed in a way that is relevant to those who have not walked along the same road. I quickly discovered that the most difficult hurdle would be to apply the seat of the pants to the seat of the chair long enough to complete the project. I cherish my privacy and I soon realized that when recorded for posterity, our lives would be exposed for permanent viewing, a thought that was more than a little intimidating, but I would not let this be a deterrent to my plan.

I loved the stories at my father's knee, tales that took the dirge out of many a winter's night. I could listen for hours to the accounts my parents told and retold, for they were pioneers who had settled in that harsh wilderness, and done battle with it for years. Their collection of folklore was a living thing because they had experienced it firsthand. Over time, new experiences, sorrows and joys have taken over the rooms where those memories had settled and cocooned, but the emotion connected to my roots is still alive. I have chosen to share some of these stories of frontiers extended and of wilderness tamed, for they have defined our past and helped shape our present. I leave it as a heritage to the next generation lest it be buried and forgotten, for I was blessed with the unprecedented privilege to experience the one-generation riptide transition from the primitive rural life to the postmodern world of technology.

Footprints of a Pioneer

In an attempt to reconcile a long overdue debt of love, I once asked my father how I could repay him for all he had done for me. His response was, "Just pass it on. That's how we got by here; we passed it on." So I invite readers to step into the past and observe what my parents passed on to me, keeping in mind that a well-written life is almost as rare as a well-spent one.

This work is not a complete biography, but merely a glimpse into our past and at the people who helped to shape our lives. It is also the spiritual journey of one woman, my mother Yvonne, who typified the many pioneer women who heroically struggled against great odds to improve living conditions for my generation. From the day she was born, this humble little pioneer followed the road of self-denial and crossed the valleys of impossibility as the chapters of her life unfolded. This is her story, intertwined with my own, and enriched with numerous anecdotes which added color to our lives, a story rich in love, laughter, and tears. I chose to omit some names to avoid embarrassing the people involved.

Now that I have some miles behind me and a few dents in my fenders, I have a better view of life and its important lessons. The people of my past are now detached figures in the corrected perspective, but they have not lost their place in my esteem, and this is my way of honoring some of them. If the bold strokes and bright colors I have used to paint these pictures create a childish image, it must be ascribed to my lack of experience as a writer and, consequently, I ask of readers a greater degree of indulgence.

Leola Meagher

The Frontier

Oh Master, let us walk with thee,
In lowly paths, in harmony
With each other, and help us bear
The strain of toil, the fret of care.

It was a warm spring day in 1935 when Yvonne came in from the garden. Her husband, Leo, was already walking up the hill from the woods. She had to hurry and cook supper, but the fire was out and she would be late.

"Calice de Tabernacle! Why isn't supper ready? I'm starving!"

"I just came in from the garden, honey."

"Don't try your sweet talk on me. The honeymoon is over. Just get on with your cooking so I can eat. I'm so hungry, my stomach thinks my throat has been cut." At these words, Yvonne relapsed into hurt silence as she coaxed the kindling into a busy blaze in the kitchen stove. She shuffled around from stove to table and back again trying to sooth her grumpy husband.

Such were the words and the attitude she would live with for the next 38 years. She had married a logger, and though she was bleeding inside, she was determined to make the best of it. Her pride kept her from sharing her grief. They had been married only six months and her laughter had already turned to tears. Where could she go for comfort? There were not many kindred spirits in their neck of the woods. Yvonne understood that, although marriages may be "made in heaven", they have to be worked out on earth, and work was taking on a whole new meaning in this new world.

Seven winding miles over the mountains to the nearest post office and general store was the homestead's only line of communication to the outside world. Leo never trekked to the village without planning a multiple of objectives, but he did not always bring Yvonne along, as he generally needed to buy cigarettes in a hurry. With this in mind, Yvonne had to make sure her letters were written in advance and her grocery list was all ready for short notice. It was to be the way of the frontier.

Why had she not foreseen this side of Leo's character? What made him so bitter? They had met in Montreal only a year before and she remembered his charming personality. Their courtship had been brief because of the economic hard times and they had decided to have a small wedding in November and immediately move north to the woodlot he had talked about. It had all sounded so logical then, but she had had no idea of the magnitude of the trials she would face along the way.

How well she remembered her trip north to her new home! The train gave a long, low growl like an anguished groan and the squealing wheels began to turn. It lurched forward, slowly picked up momentum, and hooted and chugged, rocked and whined its way along the tracks. As it threaded its way around the mountains, taking them farther from the city, Yvonne's stomach was tied in tight knots. This was wild country, entirely covered by forests like hair with the granite cliffs resembling the regrettable bald patches. Some of the mountains were solid rock walls where only hardy spruce managed to grip finger-holds in their bare flanks. All signs of civilization had been left far behind. The occasional settlement appeared isolated and lonely. How far was the frontier? Finally after many hours, with a hiss and a chug, the train made a jerky stop. They had reached their station and had to readjust themselves from the unreality of the moving train to the familiarity of feet on the ground. The young couple would cover the remaining 25 miles inland from Labelle with the mailman's horses and wagon to a settlement seven miles beyond the village of La Minerve.

She gazed at the sorry arrangement of poorly constructed buildings along the lonely road. Shabby houses had been erected wherever the owner had a mind to build. Every shack had smoke billowing from a stovepipe protruding from the roof. The train ride had been luxury compared to that lumbering wagon. As they swallowed up the miles along a rough trail into the hinterland, winding up and down around lakes and through valleys, the horses strained up steep hills and slid down the other side, the wagon and passengers bouncing along behind. It was a community painted with the brush of poverty. Yvonne thought of the pioneers who had pushed northward, casting their lonely shadows in such remote villages, their sweat on mountains and hills as they opened new frontiers. The lowering clouds sullen with snow would soon smother the moon with a gray blanket. As she watched the miles roll by, Yvonne was too weary to discipline her thoughts and too dispirited to care.

The road ended about a mile from their property, where the young couple unloaded their furniture in a neighbor's barn. Greetings were brief and Yvonne smiled a tight smile that didn't reach her eyes. They picked up their bags and hit the trail. Night had fallen and reality had begun to sink in as their steps echoed on the rocky trail, faded into the surrounding woods and died. They were covering the last lap of the 125-mile trip from Montreal into the heart of the Laurentian Mountains. They had escaped from the hopeless conditions of the urban in search of something better, a dream that was intangible and glorious, planning to carve out their own lives according to the destiny that they had perceived for themselves, a dream of freedom in a new land. That land was so mysterious, it beckoned you; yet so wild it could crush you in its treacherous grip, a great empty space of deep solitude.

The trail wound through the woods and edged the cliff toward a little cabin. It was rough and Leo guided her tenderly, respectfully, and she had been grateful for his caring attitude. They had left a mile of woods behind them when they finally reached their destination, and Yvonne realized the extent of the challenge facing her. Their new home was nothing more than a little heap of logs, 12 feet by 12 feet, in the middle of a five-acre clearing of virgin forest. In the darkness she could distinguish a roof extending beyond the walls sheltering the front door. It was simply a layer or two of slabs still wearing its bark covering. No foundation but a few rocks and posts. Their breath hung visible in the dim light of the oil lamp which revealed a rough table with two antique chairs, a wood stove, some shelves on the wall for the dishes and a double bed. For the time being, these items completed the main bulk of her earthly possessions. It was obvious that her furniture would have to remain in storage, until they could build a larger house. She bit her lip and tried to hold back the tears as the somber reality sat heavy upon her. From the heart of the city, she had been plunged overnight into the middle of the Canadian wilderness. For a moment she felt like she stood on the edge of darkness. How would she cope?

Bone-weary and dejected, Yvonne fell into a crumpled heap while Leo coaxed some kindling into a roaring fire. That first night in her new home, sleep eluded her as she lay in the darkness, listening to the kettle purring on the stove, and to the dull ticking of the clock by the bed, and all the while, wondering how she would ever manage in such cramped quarters. At last, sleep mercifully claimed her until she suddenly became aware of the clanging of the stove lids. Leo was up and lighting the fire. He had already lit a cigarette, and was shuffling about in the lamplight. At six o'clock, it was pitch black out, but Leo was preparing to feed the animals in the barn. They had been left in the care of a neighbor during his absence, and he was eager to find out how they were. Though Yvonne looked like she and sleep had never met, the young bride was expected to get up and prepare breakfast, for there would be no lounging around in this setting.

While Leo went to fetch a pail of water at the well, Yvonne pulled on some warm clothes and looked around her. What would she find by way of groceries? The faint oil lamp cast ghost shadows in the dark corners, and when her eyes had adjusted to the dim light, she moved the lamp closer to the shelves, where she discovered tins of flour, sugar, rice, lard, beans, peas, tea, molasses, and salt. She could prepare flapjacks, and hopefully, have some bread ready for supper if he had yeast. The only meat available would be salt pork, probably stored in a barrel under the floor with potatoes and root vegetables. Loggers, apparently did not sin by any excess of culinary variety.

After a hot breakfast, Leo pulled on his work clothes and headed for the woods. Yvonne washed the dishes with hot water from the kettle, and began to devise a strategy to clean up the place. "There is no use crying over spilled milk, for that will only make it salty for the cat", is a thought that crossed her mind. She would roll up her sleeves and turn this den into a home. It would prove to be a job with a rare kind of challenge. As daylight filtered through the two windowpanes on the east wall, she began to evaluate the situation. Removing the bark from the walls might be a good place to start. Whitewashing the logs would definitely brighten up the room, and a good scrubbing of the rough floor could do no harm. A tablecloth with matching curtains, and...Her imagination had quickly out-distanced the immediate task, but the possibilities were as limited as the space, so Yvonne pulled on her boots and overcoat and ventured out to look over the property.

The tiny cabin stood about 100 feet from the edge of the stern-faced rocky cliff that stood guard over the little homestead. These huge boulders formed a ridge about a hundred feet from the western boundary of the property. Beyond the dark huddle of fir trees in the hollow before her, the view to the east swept across a wide valley. The morning sky blushed as early light crept above the horizon and the sun cast its glow behind a nameless mountain like a large bump in the distance. A first snowfall covered the landscape, and in the dim light, the tree stumps and rocks strewn across the clearing looked like strange creatures hiding under a white blanket. As Yvonne stood there, acquainting herself with her new surroundings, something moved in the distance, and drifted into the shadows of the nearby forest. She had the uncanny feeling that deep in the underbrush, wild things crouched, watching her every move. Then a bluejay screamed its warnings from the shadowy vault of a nearby tree. Much to her horror, she realized that the forest on her right was uncomfortably close to the house. To make matters worse, that was precisely where Leo had built the outhouse, that brave little privy, which would withstand the rigors of wind and storm for years to come.

That brooding forest stood tall against the sky, walling in the small clearing around the cabin. The silence was deafening, the wilderness disconcerting. This new world seemed to shout to her, "You presume that you are ready to grapple with me, to tame me and polish me, but I can overpower you with my remoteness, my isolation. Think again before you settle here!" Hemmed in on every side by bare oaks and maples mingled with majestic spruce and hemlock, Yvonne shivered. Such a lonely place, where men clung to the land and wrestled with the forest, was chosen by destiny for hardy pioneers. It was a place for strong bodies and a purpose. Pioneering, she suspected, was about to rewrite the script of her life.

Her gaze moved to the little barn, a boxlike building of rough lumber erected in the bleak chaos of burned stumps. It stood to the left and below the ridge, some 300 feet away. Such was the standard of luxury that met her eyes that first day, and it was not to change any time soon. In light of the situation, Yvonne determined that very morning that she would face the challenge head on, and she wasted no time launching into the task at hand. Problems, she reasoned, are only opportunities in work clothes. She couldn't forget her vows, "for richer for poorer, for better for worse". She had carried them to the frontier, perhaps to a promise of broken dreams; yet deep in her soul she had the confidence that God's providence could sustain her there as well as anywhere else. By the time she returned to the cabin, she had herself in hand again, and the minute hand on the clock had run forward another half circle.

Winter moved in right behind them. As the days grew shorter and the nights longer, winter dragged its weight slowly across the buried hills, while the northern darkness closed in like a heavy curtain. Those first weeks were filled with emptiness as they began to lumber through long weary months. When December had set in, the snow came in drifts as the blizzards howled down with the north-easterlies. The homesteaders were held hostage for days at a time as the roads were swallowed up in the blinding, swirling snow. By the time a storm had beat itself out and the sky cleared, it left behind a cold, glittering world. The land became a barren landscape where, it seemed, only the wind was alive. The only

---

paths through the whiteness led to the well, the woodpile and the small barn. The winding dirt road that crawled across the land had disappeared under the snowdrifts, further isolating the little homestead. They were now cut off from the rest of the world by seven long miles of roadlessness.

As the stove spilled warmth through the little shack, Yvonne stared at the fitful flames and her eyes followed the smoke as it escaped into a world shimmering in the soft rays of the winter sun. In those cramped quarters, her thoughts were busy with the shadowy splendors of her dreams. She tried to follow the path of her life back to a time of laughter and hope and cringed a little as the present suddenly caught up with the past. How quiet and unselfish life could be in those days. Yet she learned to be content with small blessings and to weave gratitude into the fabric of her days. She was thankful for small mercies, such as the woodstove, the abundance of firewood, the crystal clear, cold water, food, warm clothes, and on frigid days especially for the "thunder mug" under the bed when the outhouse became completely impractical.

It was hard to believe that beneath that cold uncompromising surface, new life was stirring in preparation for all the beauty of springtime. The endless gloom of a northern winter would eventually stretch into spring when at last the sun would turn the deep snow into deep mud and the difficult winter roads would be transformed into impassible muddy ruts. But life reserved its occasional bright moments even in the dead of winter. After an ice storm, the icy road winding through the woods was like a bright necklace wrapped around the white throat of winter. When the eyes felt assaulted by the whiteness, a bluejay screamed from a tall spruce and launched across the blue expanse. On nights when the aurora borealis illuminated their dark little world, curtains of green, red and purple lights projected across the northern sky rising and falling, creating a fantasy of breathtaking beauty. These displays surpassed even that of the full moon that bathed their dark world in the soft radiance of her glow. Morning was perhaps the most astonishing time of day when the growing light wrestled the shadows from the dark undergrowth of the surrounding forest.

There was also the gloomy side of winter when the moonlight cast eerie shadows across the field. From the dark recesses of the forest echoed mournful howls. Through the darkness of thick woods, here and there pierced by the moonlight, the wolves moved swiftly and silently in the deep snow. The noiseless journeying continued following the scent of their prey through the forest. At the edge of the clearing, they paused close to a cabin bathed in the glare of the full moon. The smell of man held them back. Peeking out the little window, Yvonne was startled to see a large herd of deer shivering in the night. These beautiful animals had sought shelter in the little clearing by her home. She prayed for their safety, and lay in bed wondering about this wild country. Those savage howls sliced the stillness like a knife and brought goose bumps as Yvonne was reminded of the distance that separated them from civilization. They had settled on the backside of nowhere. Of course the luxuries of a telephone and electricity would have to await the building of a good road, the ultimate civilizing weapon. Would she ever put down roots? Could this strange world become her home?

There was plenty of time to entertain such thoughts as the dim winter dragged on in the little cabin. Some days she felt that she had no neighbor but the wind. Yvonne craved to give time a shove. Besides cooking salt pork and potatoes, baking bread and biscuits and washing the two cups and two plates after every meal, she had to stoke the fire, carry in the firewood, occasionally feed the ox and cow in the tiny barn and fetch water from the well when Leo was away. The well had the major inconvenience of being located down the hill from the cabin, making laundry a challenge anytime, but a real battle in the winter months. The pump handle was so cold on frigid mornings that even with woolen mittens, her hands complained. When the road surface turned to ice, hauling those heavy buckets up the slope presented new perils.

It was on such a trek that Yvonne fell and had her first of six miscarriages alone on the frontier. There was no point to grieving in idleness. She was learning that when life gets in the way of dreams, one must go on. Doctors seldom traveled to their neck of the woods for obvious reasons. Roads were often closed, and without a telephone, it was always guesswork to locate the good doctor whose house calls covered an area nearly the size of Montreal. Under the circumstances, most people learned to cope as best they could with home remedies. Most babies were born long before the doctor arrived and usually a neighbour learned midwifery on the spot as life carried on for those brave folk.

Without so much as a radio in those early days, what did people do for entertainment? Because the weather set the rules for these pioneers, when a country community was snowbound, it was held within itself and folks created their own entertainment. After days of weather-induced confinement, on Saturday evenings, families gathered in different homes, sat around the kitchen table and played cards by lamplight. They laughed at their recycled jokes, argued, told stories, or passed on bits of information and old news that had been distorted and embellished by repetition. As stories traveled along this vast territory with the speed of the bush telegraph, they gained in drama and momentum, adding to the entertainment. These informal gatherings served as a safety valve to relieve stress and renew friendships. It proved to be a way of escape that helped to prevent arthritis of the soul. Children were part of these happy gatherings until they fell asleep on a chair in the corner, or on the floor by the stove with the dog or cat. Life was not complicated for the young back then.

Sundays were set aside for rest and restoration. Folks usually slowed their pace, and even the horses were left in the stable to rest on the Sabbath. Leo sometimes went to the village, where he attended Mass and picked up his mail and some groceries. The back doors were left open to accommodate those who lived far away. When the roads were closed after a snowstorm or during the spring thaw, Leo skied or snow-shoed those seven miles. That trek would be a challenge for any athlete, but to cover the distance with a heavy backpack of groceries might not be a sportsman's idea of fun. After the first downhill plunge, the terrain was flat for a couple of miles, followed by an uphill climb for over three miles before heading down again in a twisting, undulating, cross-country bobsled run along a narrow, tree-lined road. If he fell, he would carry the battle scars to show for it. His errands completed, the daunting return journey stood before him. Even in brutally cold temperatures, his steady pace kept him in a lather, as he traveled that picturesque trail mile after long mile. Exhausted, his skis dragged along with little enthusiasm, as he descended the last hills before the long ascent towards their isolated settlement and the promise of a hot supper by the stove.

Months and years passed, filled with hard work, heavy disappointments, and occasional deep joys. For Yvonne, life was like a sea without markers in terms of time and space and change. Through their endless struggles, she was demonstrating traits of fortitude, strength and optimism. In her letters, it was hard to describe that wild country, and explain its isolation and complete absence of civilized comforts. Then looking around, she concluded that perhaps she was nearer to God here than anywhere else.

Sweat and Tears

Leo with Charlie, in 1934.

Leo and Puppy, in 1933.

Yvonne's first home: 1934 to 1937.

Clearing the virgin forest: 1933 - 1940.

Sweat and Tears

Troubles work patience,
and patience, experience
and experience, hope. (Romans 5:3-5)

Because the woods were omnipresent, it was a challenge for the pioneer to open a parenthesis wide enough to build a house. When the ax had intimidated the forest into submission, a cluster of small buildings sprouted on succeeding lots along the dirt roads, pushing back the tree line little by little. These isolated dwellings hovelled in mute despair, silent witnesses to the poverty that dwelt within. The world was groaning under extreme economic hopelessness, and they were groaning with it. Life was hard for Yvonne, but even more brutal for Leo who struggled and laboured from pre-dawn into the dark of night to eke out a living in that unforgiving country. In his constant struggle, he used a number of theological words, but he didn't put them together in a theological manner. Too poor to afford a horse that first winter, he worked with an ox, Charlie by name. In spite of his harsh words and grumpy attitude, Leo was kind to his animals and Charlie proved to be a good source of power. The trouble with a steer is that its endurance doesn't match its strength, and Charlie had to stop often to catch his breath when pulling a heavy load.

Equipped with only hand saws and an axe, felling hardwood trees, stripping off the branches, and sawing the trunks into three-foot lengths was a challenge for any man; but in deep snow the task was exhausting. To split a three-foot log of maple took skill and incredible strength. This firewood then had to be stacked and ready to move before the spring thaw. In order to move the many cords of wood out of the forest to a main road, the logger had to carve out a winter road through the forest following the general slope of the land along frozen waterways or valleys downhill. A large sleigh, usually homemade, was stacked high with logs and the team of horses or oxen pulled these heavy loads several miles down to the loading platforms, where they would be hauled by train to the city to fuel furnaces and heat large buildings. Loggers were always at the mercy of the elements and an early thaw could spell disaster. Worse still, exploitation walked those country roads following the pioneers to their very doorstep.

Leo worked in the stillness of the woods where nature makes no strident noises, regardless of the vastness of the operation. The sounds were quiet and harmonious, a music that was as old as the world, the sound of the wind through the trees, the howl of a wolf. Only the sound of the snow squeaking beneath his felt mukluks broke the silence of the land. The suffocating cold was like a wild beast trying to creep deep into his clothing to feed on his body heat. At the edge of the woods, Leo removed the frost from his eyelashes with his mittened hand. His still form was dwarfed by the ancient trees, reigning unchallenged as they had for countless ages. This was virgin land whose days as an uninhabited territory were numbered. He had the feeling that a privileged communion with nature permitted him to look upon a world that had remained secret and solitary since ancient times. He surveyed the vast whiteness he had just crossed before entering the gloom of the forest. A logger lived from his childhood in communion with the woods from the Siberian winter days through the tropical summer heat. In those vast forests, it was easy for a logger to lose his way and, more than once, Leo had that gut-wrenching experience. On one occasion, he had been aiming to walk out of a logging camp to reach a neighboring village at night. Only it was so dark that the only way out had been to walk in the middle of a stream.

As was the custom, all this was accomplished with a smoldering cigarette glued to his lower lip. With such primitive equipment, it is little wonder the man dragged himself home exhausted and grumpy and it wasn't long before Yvonne noted that Leo's short temper soured a little more under tobacco deprivation. When the long winter ended and the beautiful spring weather finally arrived, the loggers were defenseless against swarms of mosquitoes and black flies that declared all-out war, attacking like fighter jets. More than once, Leo suggested that pioneers should consider changing vocation from raising beef to raising flies: the massive, fleshy kind.

Life held little to smile about in the darkness of the times and before long, the freshness and vigor of youth had left his face. Night had scarcely sneaked over the hill for fear of the rising sun when the rooster crowed to introduce another day. Even before daybreak, it seemed the day's work reached out and grabbed him, and the days never ended; they were nothing but a series of events separated by darkness. Tomorrow promised only to resemble today and yesterday, an endless cycle of economic despair. Leo's life was dictated by the surrounding woods and all its moods. His was a world of forest and skies on which the sun rose every morning and the stars and moon each night and always. But the other option was unemployment in the city and line-ups at the soup kitchens. Leo's pride would never allow him to beg for his living. Logging was still a more noble business in his eyes. In those circumstances, he knew that he could not be rich, but he would be known as a man of integrity, a quality he never lived to regret.

L'ANNONCIATION, le 7 novembre 1946.

A TOUS LES COLONS

RE:- COUPE DE BOIS

Cher monsieur,

Pour faire suite au désir de l'Honorable Ministre de la Colonisation, il me fait plaisir de vous faire part des nouvelles instructions concernant la coupe de bois sur les lots de colonisation:

Le Ministre de la Colonisation, l'Honorable J.-D. Bégin, désireux d'encourager le développement agricole sur les lots des colons et d'aider ceux-ci à assurer un établissement stable et permanent pour leur famille, demande la coopération de tous les officiers de son Ministère pour surveiller et contrôler la coupe du bois sur les lots de colonisation.

Aucun bois ne doit être coupé en dehors des défrichements.

Le permis accordé ne devra jamais dépasser 30,000 pmp ou 60 cordes. Cependant, si vous constatez que dans les cinq acres que ce colon a à défricher, il y a plus de bois que la quantité mentionnée plus haut, vous pourrez donner un autre permis qui couvrira la balance du bois à couper.

Aucun permis ne sera accordé à un colon qui a fait du bois les années précédentes et qui, au cours de l'été, n'a pas fait d'améliorations et de défrichement nouveau et profitable sur son lot.

Espérant que tous les colons voudront bien se conformer à ces instructions,

Bien à vous,

HENRI FORTIER, inspecteur

N.B. Les colons qui ont commencé des coupes en dehors des abatis devront cesser de couper immédiatement.
                    H.F.

Fighting the System

When times are dark, the struggles grim,
And cares rise like a flood,
Together we can face the foe,
Together we can win.

Both Yvonne and Leo were slaves of the times and both struggled to break those shackles and improve their lot. They understood that the only place "success" comes before "work" is in the dictionary. Dreams began with the words, "When I sell my wood in the spring, we can buy... and I'll build....", but the price of cordwood barely fetched enough to pay the grocery and feed bills. There was seldom money left over to see even the humblest dream become reality during those years of the great depression.

Those who have never been slaves have never really tasted freedom. And looking back over their lives, I realize that theirs was a world of disillusionment, a succession of broken dreams. I am convinced that freedom burns more deeply in the heart of a man from whom freedom has been stolen. It was that burning desire to break out of the endless cycle of poverty, that burned deep in the hearts of those pioneers, known as "les Colons" in rural Quebec. The Quebec government of the day had devised a system called "Colonisation" with the purpose of populating the vast empty territory of the province. People were assigned a woodlot of perhaps 100 acres with certain conditions attached. Until such conditions were met, the government remained part owner of the land. The settler had to clear 30% of the land and plow for cultivation a minimum of 10%, while logging a limited quota in winter to earn a living. The problem lay in the type of land. The lot could be on a steep mountainside with rocky soil, making it totally impossible to farm. Those settlers who managed to raise dairy cattle could not deliver their milk or cream because of the lamentable road conditions. In the remote settlements, there was neither telephone nor electricity; roads remained closed for long periods in winter and any request for improvement was met with resistance and sometimes, vigorous opposition, depending on one's political allegiance.

Leo was of small stature. His 5-feet, 7-inch frame was solid muscle, but his weight never exceeded 150 pounds all dressed. He worked off the calories as soon as Yvonne cooked them on. Exposure to sun and wind had etched lines at the corners of his dark eyes, giving a marked intensity to his expression. What energy he did not spend extracting logs from the forest or mowing hay in the clearings, he concentrated on fighting the "System". With each election campaign, a new kind of passion engulfed him. A driving obsession for reform, or just to stir things up seemed a great reward in itself. It was a futile battle that raged and coursed through his veins. At times his mind was filled with the flames of anger and the blackness of resentment, but he refused to let their grinding poverty depress him. He would fight it, even if it meant taking on the world. As he wrestled to find a loophole in the solid wall of officialdom, he felt like a field mouse cornered by a very large snake. All the while, Leo was weighted to the drudgery of the farm like one of the great boulders dominating the ridge beyond the barn. He had yet to learn that those who opposed that colonial regime were hard-put to reform its evil ways. The bureaucrats of the old order spoke in loud and imperative tones when they dealt with pioneers. Whether they ever really understood the genuine problems of these brave folk must remain an academic question.

Sometimes it was not clear which made him angrier, the blind acceptance by the population of their lot or their exploitation by the Duplessis regime. He was convinced that fear of change caused some people to be comfortable in their misery, secure in their mediocrity and paralyzed in their prejudice. His savage temper was a vital weapon of survival in that never-ending battle. Yvonne recalled Leo's sarcasm aimed at his oppressors: "How many more backward steps can people take before falling off the edge of relevance and into the black hole of stupidity!" Such explosions were often accompanied by a string of cuss words borrowed from the furnishings of the Roman Catholic Church. His favorite was "calice" and went like this: "calice de misere" or "calice de pays". Yvonne was used to these outbursts. It was the stuff of their lives. After all, it is a well-known fact that loggers, (les bûcherons) learned to cuss before they learned to walk. It was a built-in safety valve to diffuse frustration and anger in a setting where power knows little justice.

On one occasion, Yvonne had to deal with a bureaucrat who fancied he knew all about the settlers' problems from the comfort of his lofty post. They did not know each other before that visit and, I suspect they never forgot each other since. He was a long, thin, pale-faced man with thinning hair and a prominent forehead. He seemed to be carrying his own gloom, for his tall, gaunt figure was made even longer by a long overcoat. It was obvious that she did not have a very exalted opinion of the virtues of these delegates from head-quarters. The topic had provoked a strong weather pattern in her mind, and after repeated attempts to explain the dilemma they were facing, and after a loaded silence, she lost all self-control and blurted out: "You appear to carry your intelligence where our hens keep their eggs, somewhere in the lower regions!" That man's eyes opened wide, his eyebrows went out of sight, and he went speechless. Never before had anyone questioned his intellect. Needless to say, Yvonne had not helped her cause that day and it would be an understatement to add that the offended party never repeated his visits. At times, anger battled with despair when there was no one to connect with to channel her complaints. On many occasions they wrote letters only to have their hopes dashed and continue their struggle with nothing in their pockets but broken dreams. Yet in spite of repeated reversals, they refused to do business with defeat, and simply carried on.

Bertha

For all the heartaches and the tears,
For gloomy days and fruitless years,
I do give thanks, for now I know
These were the things that helped me grow.

For Yvonne, the future pattern of their lives was clearly emerging, and a lifetime of loneliness yawned before her. Surely God had a greater purpose for her life than this monotony. Months dragged into years and her empty arms ached for children. In God's economy, it seems that time is as important as speed, yet she was confident that someday the Lord would answer her prayer for a baby.

In the meantime, Yvonne always kept busy, and with her creative spirit, she concentrated her energy on a variety of projects. The first winter, she moved her sewing machine from a neighbour's barn where her furniture was in storage, into the tiny cabin where she took it upon herself to design and sew winter clothes for the children of a large family on a neighbouring homestead. She skilfully took apart winter overcoats and other used clothing they had received from folks in the city, and proceeded to cut out and sew children's snowsuits. If a garment did not fit one child, it was sure to fit another, as those precious little children came in all sizes, a new one every year or two. With the remnants, she assembled quilts to fit the many beds in their cold frame house. Such activities took the edge off her loneliness.

As she pedaled that old machine, the wood stove wrapped her in its warmth. The crackling of the fire was a melody that blended with the song in her heart. It was as though she poured her soul into every garment she sewed as a love offering to those in need. Alone with the heavy kettle purring in a pleasantly domestic fashion, the hours ticked away. She had managed to occupy every square inch of the tiny cabin by adding to the clutter that was its normal burden. Should visitors drop in, they would have to sit on the bed; but such a treat was a rare occurrence in the dead of winter.

One day, shortly after her arrival in the wilderness, Yvonne had a visitor. She was an old German woman who had negotiated the rough trail through the woods to the little cottage in the clearing. The dear soul spoke precious little English, and Yvonne's knowledge of the king's language was just as limited, but it was their only common lingo. The two sat together over a cup of tea, exchanging messages in sign language sprinkled with the occasional word of mutilated English that might have sounded like this: "Zince I gott up dis mornin' I don't feel so goot." And the response, "You like cup a tea?" Hugs and tears revealed clear understanding where words failed. In the months that followed, Yvonne's new friend repeated her visits, bringing her a rose bush, and various perennial plants to add to her little garden in the spring. Being very sensitive, Yvonne had the feeling that, in order to rise above despair, this woman yearned for something lost that had to be retrieved before time ran out. Nevertheless, that lady's kindness brought a ray of sunshine into her otherwise lonely existence.

On one such visit the following summer, her friend tried to tell Yvonne about her daughter Bertha, but Yvonne thought she was talking about a doctor and wondered if she was sick. Thoroughly confused, she asked Leo to explain, and this is the sad story that fell on the pregnant hush of the garden that evening, a tale that has remained etched in my memory since the day Mama shared it with us many years later.

When Bertha was sixteen, sometime after World War I, she arrived in Canada from Germany to join the rest of her family in time for Christmas. Everything was so new and exciting that even the primitive conditions of the settlement could not disappoint her. On Christmas Eve, her brother Theodore took her out to buy groceries at the general store, 25 miles away. They set out before daybreak in a one-horse sleigh to make the return trip the same day. The day was uneventful as the horse cantered along the lonely road over the mountains. The tinkling bells on the harness conjured up happy memories and brought a smile to Bertha's face as she reveled in the happiness of her first Christmas in Canada. Together they laughed and reminisced about the good old days back home so long ago. Several hours had passed, when houses appeared more frequently, and they knew that they were nearing their destination.

At the store, the horse was parked in the shelter and covered with a heavy blanket, where it could rest and be fed and watered. There were other customers packing their sleighs with more extravagance than usual, with apples and oranges packed lovingly in cardboard boxes beside little buckets of hard candy. Red and green ribbons decked the store window with a large bell in the center. The kind merchant invited his customers to warm up by the pot-bellied stove in the middle of the floor. To the men, he offered a generous glass of homemade brew, they called moonshine; to the ladies hot tea by way of hospitality. Theodore raised his glass to the ladies and drank heartily as Bertha handed her list to the grocer behind the counter and warmed her hands by the fire. The shelves to her left were a multicolored cornucopia of fabric, ribbons and houseware. The space behind the counter on the right was occupied with drawers and shelves containing bulk food, like flour, sugar, and beans. The meat was kept in a cold room in the back storage, and the fruit was displayed in the counter.

The man measured and weighed and packed the sugar, flour, beans, peas, tea, spices and dried fruit in boxes, adding a little extra candy for the children. Bertha helped to pick out some pretty fabric and a few little gifts for the family, while Theodore added tobacco and kerosene to the order, and collected the mail for the entire neighbourhood. When their feet had finally thawed out and all the items were packed and carefully loaded onto the sleigh, they set out for the long trek back. The sun was already dipping low on the horizon, and they would have to travel long into the night.

All wrapped in a buffalo skin, Bertha snuggled up to Theodore. This was the brother she had missed so terribly since he had left Germany before the war. She had remained behind with her cousins until her family could book passage for her later. There was so much to talk about, as their conversation resumed and fluttered from one topic to another. Then, quite abruptly, Theodore began to squirm and complain of stomach cramps and a sharp pain in his abdomen. He handed the reins to his sister and moved to the back of the sleigh, where he lay down under a heavy blanket.

Night had fallen under a clear December sky and, as the cold intensified, Bertha's hands and feet grew numb. The horse kept a steady pace, producing little puffs of steam not unlike a locomotive nosing along a winding track. The snow squeaking beneath the runners in time with the puffs had a hypnotizing effect. Mile after mile of wilderness stretched before her in the dim light of the new moon, and the solitude was frightening. Dark shadows began moving in her imagination and she was sure she heard wolves howling in the distance.

Feeling sleep overtaking her, Bertha reined in the horse to wake up her brother. He could take over while she slept. She shook him, but to her horror, he did not respond. He was cold and stiff. The frigid night suddenly became oppressive and she felt the woods closing in on her. She felt trapped as the landscape threatened to disappear. Death had thieved its way into her life. Theodore was ... a corpse! "Oh God, this can't be!" But the little horse could detect the presence of death and grew restless. He began to snort and, without warning lurched forward, throwing his stunned passenger to the floor of the sleigh. Badly shaken, Bertha grabbed the reins of the runaway horse, a German girl in a foreign land with the corpse of her brother as her only companion.

Dazed, she kept going until she spotted a light in the distance. There she finally drove the horse into the lane and pounded on the door. The startled folks ushered her into their house in a cloud of frosty air, but could not understand her frantic pleas for help in German. Bertha led them to the sleigh, where she uncovered her dead brother. As the reality of the tragedy hit them, these kind folks tried to console the young stranger. Together they unloaded the stiff body and laid it down in the safety of the woodshed for the night. While the man took the horse to the barn, the woman led their distraught guest into the house and made up a bed for her to spend the night, that dreadful night when the cold hand of death had snatched the brother she loved, and with him, her very childhood.

When the night wore on and Theodore and Bertha had not returned, the family's apprehensions grew, but there was little they could do at that late hour. Then early Christmas morning, the sleigh finally appeared, carrying a single passenger. A second sleigh followed and the stranger helped Bertha to the door. As the tragic story unfolded, the scene became chaotic and Bertha collapsed from exhaustion.

Christmas had never again been a happy occasion for the old lady. Not only had she lost a son, Bertha decided to return to Germany, unable to settle in the land that had brought so much tragedy into her life. As Yvonne reflected on this sad story, she wondered what the future held in store for them. Would they also become the victims of food poisoning, disease, or a severe accident? Should an emergency arise, help would never reach them in time. They had to throw themselves on the mercy of the Almighty. In most cases people resorted to home remedies, some so potent that it seemed self-evident that any bacillus that could survive these recipes had to be super bugs, and any patient who could survive the treatment probably had little to fear from the infection.

Attack Dog

It has been said that the most persistent sound reverberating down through the ages is the beating of war drums. The 1930's economic depression was only a brief moment of partial peace in history when everyone stood around reloading. Then 1939 confirmed peoples' fears and started the worst conflict in human history. Young soldiers from the colonies were sent to the front lines where they soon lay beneath the carnage of that vicious conflict. Even the pioneers in remote communities were not untouched. For Yvonne it brought a new sorrow. Her youngest brother, the one she had raised from infancy and called "Ti Gars" (Little boy), was training recruits in Halifax with the 22nd Regiment. He would eventually leave for Europe to fight the Nazis in Belgium.

Many young men, detecting the seeds of doom in Germany's rising militarism, emigrated to the New World. A first wave of these immigrants settled in our remote community in the years preceding and immediately following World War I. Others joined them later and the settlement became known as Little Germany. Their resettlement, however, did not extinguish their patriotism for the Fatherland, as Leo was to discover firsthand.

When Hitler, the mad leader of the Nazis, had locked the entire German culture into an unstoppable treadmill of war, some of our German neighbours became strong Nazi sympathizers. On several occasions, when Leo walked by their house, they mimed the Nazi salute or drank a toast to Hitler. Well-oiled with alcohol, they sang derogatory songs about the French.

"Ils sont dans l'fosset

Les P'tits Français.

Ha ha ha ha!

Leo's sense of humour did not extend that far and he clearly resented these outbursts. He was often tempted to throw off the thin cloak of civility that covered his short temper and blast them royally, but he held back. To add insult to injury, their dog usually ran out from under a wagon snarling viciously and threatening to bite him. Leo warned the owner to control his hound, but the man thought it was hilarious and rattled on about its Nazi temperament.

About that time, it happened that Leo's she-dog was in heat, and who should defect to his property but that infamous hound. It was payback time. He snatched his leather horsewhip from the barn as the dog lunged at him, snarling very dirty words in dog language. Death stood naked in his eyes. Leo cracked the whip over the animal's back. In a flash, the hound grabbed it and bit off the end. Leo saw red, and what he lacked in size, he made up for in fury. Spewing a mouthful of ripe language, he picked up a chain, determined to teach that vicious creature a lesson to remember. The hound crouched, ready to spring at his opponent's throat, but Leo was able to dodge the first leap and responded with a series of lashes across the dog's back. He had to beat the dog into submission, whipping it until it had ceased its snarling and came crawling up to lick his hand. At last it conceded defeat at the hands of a new master who commanded respect. Such was Leo's temperament and sense of justice. He believed that a vicious animal does not deserve to live. "Chien qui mord merite la mort." That dog limped home with less hair, more bruises, and a different attitude.

The next time he walked past that property, the dog went into hiding, provoking Leo's comment, "Have you been feeding your dog too much chicken lately?" 1945 saw the mad dreams of the Nazi regime, which had sought to conquer the free world, disperse in the dust and ashes of a ruined Germany. They had failed to destroy freedom, and those neighbours were no longer German. They had all become Czechoslovakian, and Hitler had lost much of his popularity. The short-wave radios that had been used for spying had disappeared into the woodwork and since then, little has been said about the Nazis in these parts.

The Bully

The bigger they come,
The harder they fall.

When loggers sold cordwood (three-foot long split firewood), they received half the payment when the wood was stacked at the railroad siding and the remainder when the wood was delivered. There was usually a middle man who took care of marketing the wood in the city. Such a man who lived in Mont Laurier, was known as the bully of the county. Most of the loggers had to deal with him.

When that dealer drove up to their neck of the woods, Leo asked him when he intended to pay him the balance he still owed him from the previous winter. The big man rolled down the car window and responded in his usual condescending style: "I don't care to pay assholes." That was a big mistake, because the brute had underestimated the wiry man he had foolishly insulted. Leo had been an amateur boxer in his youth and logging kept him in top shape. Of small stature, he had two weapons at his disposal, his quick temper and his fists, and both were lethal. Before he had time to roll up his window, Leo landed his first punch and broke the guy's nose. Provoked and bleeding, the angry giant burst out of his vehicle to retaliate, but Leo's fists were more than he had bargained for. That bundle of fury gave him the whipping of his life and left his limp form in a heap beside his car. Apparently the bully's eyes were both swollen shut and, unable to drive his car, he stumbled some two miles to have a local nurse bandage him up until he could pick up his car the following day. When he returned to his headqurters, he was hard-put to explain his "accidental" encounter. Though I am not sure whether Leo was ever paid for his many weeks of hard labour, word soon got around that intimidation could be risky business around loggers.

That incident took place on a Sunday afternoon and when

Leo walked home, his white shirt covered in blood, Yvonne suspected a settling of accounts. Would her husband never learn to use diplomacy instead of his fists as a tool of persuasion? He had to explain that he had had the satisfaction of teaching a bully a lesson that he would not soon forget. "It is not the size of the dog in the fight, but the size of the fight in the dog that determines the victory." Bullies are proverbial cowards and it took the courage of one man to step out and defend a whole community from exploitation. It was said that the men were paid more promptly after that incident.

Yvonne's Childhood

When tomorrow comes and trials beat
upon your castle walls,
Remember the healing power of laughter deeply shared,
And hold on to those things that are important
As you walk into the unknown and face new cares.

At last the long biting months of winter were dissolving in the clean-washed days of April. The woods were vibrant with the stirring of life, for spring had finally come to the little homestead. To greet the month of May, the world had slipped on its loveliest attire, a soft green dress dotted with yellow dandelions, white trilliums, and blue violets. In fact, the days of May that year could have been borrowed from June, so warm and bright were they. Swallows skimmed in brave abandon the swollen waters of a flooded hollow. When Yvonne stepped outside, a riot of sound greeted her. God's little orchestra made the air vocal with their melody. Yvonne smiled as she listened to that symphony of warbling songbirds in the teaming attics of the surrounding woods. Her world was alive with music. Each morning when Leo left for the woods, she walked out to see the sun rise over the mountain. The flush reddened, the world yawned and a new day was born, a day full of possibilities.

Yvonne gloried in each sun-splashed new day, breathing in the newborn spring. One day, she decided to explore the clearing to the north of the cabin. She discovered a trail that threaded its way up the steep hillside. It led to a tiny cascade that passed through a castle-like heap of boulders hidden in the woods, skipping and gurgling its musical way over the rocky hillside where wild flowers bloomed in fragile beauty and birdsong gave descant to the tumbling waterfall. The air was full of the scent of ferns, damp soil and dead leaves. When she walked back to her house, there was a bounce in her step for the world was new and full of promise.

It was time to plant a garden, an essential source of food for the months ahead. As Leo helped her turn the rich loam, she fertilized it with manure and lovingly planted the precious seeds in straight rows where the plants would receive the most sun. Whenever anyone approached the garden, Yvonne was visible only as a flowered cotton rump above the tomato plants. Surprised, she up-ended to her full five feet to welcome her guests. The weeding and watering would keep her busy all summer, but she determined that there was more to gardening than vegetables. She would add beauty to her little cottage with flowers. Armed with a variety of morning glories, sweet peas and other seeds, she planted a garden like no other. These creepers and vines soon covered and engulfed with their moist green leaves and colorful blooms every square inch of the log walls, reaching up to the roof to wrap even the stovepipe, ending in tiny spirals waving up to the sky. Yvonne had to tie back that wild curtain on either side of the window and door to let the light pass into the cabin. People came from miles around to visit that unusual little house on the hill wearing a summer dress, perhaps recalling a far-away garden in the morning of time.

During the brief summer months when Leo was away working on the railroad, Yvonne's younger sisters took turns visiting her. Those were happy times of reminiscing, gardening and laughing together. Time each morning seemed to be sliding on greased skids. When the animals were fed, the milking done, the milk separated and the cream cooled, breakfast had fit in somewhere and the dishes were washed. The music of the woods echoed her mood as she hummed to the rhythm of the little churn filled with fresh cream. The girls recalled their childhood on a large dairy farm in the Eastern Townships. Theirs had been a happy family of eleven children raised after Quebec tradition. Those memories were like lost pieces of herself floating in from her past.

Grandpapa had been a fiddler and the life of every party, and Yvonne recalled the many celebrations where she had accompanied his songs on the piano. Everyone loved Delphis and his jovial personality. Christmas-time, known as

Yvonne's Childhood

"Le Temps des Fetes" in French Canada, could be summed up as a succession of parties beginning with Christmas Eve midnight mass followed by "le reveillon" and continuing through Epiphany on January 6. These took the form of gatherings in various homes of relatives and neighbours where tables groaned with food and people sang and danced to the tunes of lively folk music on the fiddles, accordions, spoons, harmonicas and sometimes a piano. A little home-brewed moonshine added to the happy mood and raised the volume of the songs. Those were the days when even toddlers were included in the festivities, and simply put to bed in the course of the evening when they ran out of steam. The rest of the company continued to celebrate into the wee hours of the morning.

Sometimes the men of the house disappeared with a lantern to do the early morning milking while the women prepared a hefty breakfast of flapjacks for everyone before these families dispersed with horses and sleighs into the frigid morning. Sleigh runners squeaked and bells tinkled as the horses cantered along, homeward bound, blowing little puffs of steam into the crisp winter air. As Yvonne remembered those days of long ago, she felt as though she were being touched by the very edge of happiness.

Her life had not been all sunshine and delight, for even as a child, she had been assigned a heavy load of responsibility. When she was five years old, her father decided that she was big enough to milk a cow; so Yvonne had been assigned a gentle animal in the large dairy herd. Her little hands soon developed the strength necessary to squirt out a whole bucket of milk morning and evening. With each additional birthday, another cow was added to her work detail. Such were the customs of rural life in the early 1900's. But even those memories did not bring regret, for these had been wholesome activities shared by many other children of the day.

Yvonne remembered the day her papa had taken her to town with the horse and sleigh the week before Christmas. She was six that year and had never seen anything so grand before. As they walked along the main street at dusk, festive lights spilled across the glistening road like liquid gold. The tinsel-framed windows enticed and entranced her with their Christmas magic. It was all too much to take in and she felt queasy with anticipation. She couldn't recall the object of their trip, but remembered the day as a huge adventure and how the cold air smote like a hammer blow when they left the warmth of the bright shops to return home in the cold winter night. Their own village was cocooned in velvet blackness with small shops that appeared to be candlelit in comparison to the dazzling brightness of downtown Sherbrooke.

Being the oldest daughter in the family was not a rank to be envied. In 1916, when she was 12 years old, Yvonne had taken over the entire household for several weeks following the birth of another little brother. She had to cook, bake bread, clean house, and do laundry for 13 people, including the farm hands. Over the years, her mother often insisted that she stay home from school to help her in the house. Poor Yvonne loved learning and pleaded in vain with her mama to let her go to school. It is amazing that, in spite of her erratic attendance, she produced excellent grades and successfully completed tenth grade in 1920.

It was sometime after Yvonne left the convent that she met a young man from a nearby village. It was not that he exactly disturbed her, but simply that his attentions were so absorbing. She became fond of him and attempted to explain to her parents that he was different from any man she had ever known. He respected her and valued her opinions unlike most young men who sought to exploit the romantic side. Much to her dismay, they firmly objected to his friendship because he was protestant. Such a liaison was frowned upon as totally inappropriate for a catholic girl. The pain left in her heart made her cautious of new associations.

At that time she had to discontinue her studies in order to help support the family because her father was seriously ill. When he had become too sick to work the farm, Delphis had sold all the animals at auction and moved the family from St-Edwidge to Coaticook, where the older children might find jobs. Months passed and her dad grew worse. The year was 1924 when, following a prolonged illness, Delphis Petit died of prostate cancer at age 53, leaving behind a widow with ten children. Poor Grand-maman had never so much as paid a bill in her entire life, so busy had she been bearing and raising children. The money from the farm auction had gone to pay the doctor's bills and support the family during her husband's sickness. She was left with one thousand dollars from life insurance and ten children, the youngest a three-year-old toddler.

As the girls reminisced, Yvonne remembered the tough years that followed the family's move to Montreal. Well-meaning relatives had advised Grand-maman to move to the city where the older children could find good paying jobs and learn trades that would help support the family. Of course, no one had foreseen the impending economic depression of the 1930's and little did they realize the struggles that lay ahead.

The family could afford only a modest flat in the poorest neighbourhood of St-Henri; and when the threat of eviction came knocking at the front door, Grandmaman moved the family out the back door, often in the night to seek shelter elsewhere. These were dark times for the poor. It was only in the winged freedom of her reading that Grand-maman was able to find release from the daily grind and dark despair of their poverty. One day she wrote the following poem about her house, the spacious farmhouse they had left behind in their quest for riches in the city several years before:

MA MAISON

Cette nuit, vous l'avouerais-je
Je suis allée là-bas vers cet horizon
Ou s'écoulaient jadis mes jours sans nuages,
Et j'ai revu ma maison, notre chère maison,
Ou longtemps nous avons joui d'un bonheur
sans partage.

J'allai d'abord m'agenouiller près du berceau.
C'est là, en vérité, que j'ai vécu mes jours les plus beaux.
Combien de fois, tous deux, au-dessus penchés,
Votre père et moi, avec amour, avons épié

Vos premiers sourires et recueilli vos baisers.

Je me dirigeai ensuite vers la grande salle
Ou confusément j'entendais comme un bruit de bal;
Ses murs détonnaient, de l'absent les joyeuses chansons.
Ravie, j'écoutais avec dévotion,
Lorsque de jolis accords me firent tourner la tête,
Et j'aperçus Rose au piano accompagnant
ses frères au violon.
Que c'était beau! Que c'était émouvant,
Cette réception pour mon époux et mes chers enfants.

Mais tout cet enchantement cessa
Quand des mains d'Oscar son violon se brisa
Et c'est un deuil
Que j'ai repassé toute seule!
Je me retrouvais près de l'âtre
Ou les cendres éteintes s'amassent;
Avec les pincettes, longtemps je les ai remuées.
J'y ai fait surgir des souvenirs tristes, d'autres gais;
Mais tous, ils m'ont fait pleurer.

Mes larmes, tout à coup s'arrêtèrent,
Les yeux agrandis, je regarde avec défi
Ces petites figures étrangères
Qui autour de moi rient.
Voilà que je les entends se dirent :
'Qu'a-t-elle donc, cette vieille à venir pleurer ici?'
Et je suis parti, sans me retourner.
Par : A. B. Petit

A day came when there was no food for her family and no
money. What was she to do? As a faithful Roman Catholic,
she walked to the local church, an immense stone structure,
to ask the priest for help. Begging was humiliating, but she
had no other option in her dilemma. When she knocked at
the door, expecting kindness and understanding, the priest
looked down his nose at her and asked her what she had
done with her money when she had some. Then he took 10

cents out of his pocket and handed it to her. Totally overwhelmed with grief, she cried all the way home. She felt like she stood on the edge of darkness, so deep was her despair. When she poured her heart out to a neighbour, the kind lady told her about the Salvation Army. She assured Grand-maman that these good people would help her regardless of her religion. To her utter amazement, the same day total strangers delivered a large box of groceries, more than she had ever imagined, no questions asked. That day she and her family learned two wonderful truths; that God had not forgotten them, and that perhaps The Lord was not exclusively Roman Catholic after all. Mama told me that this incident led to Grand-maman's quest for the truth by reading the scriptures, which had always been forbidden by her church.

The only jobs available to young women in those lean years were as maids in wealthy households in affluent neighborhoods like Westmount. So Yvonne put aside her independent spirit and conceded to don the little starched apron and bonnet to serve the rich and hand over her menial salary to feed her brothers and sisters. A job that had been advertised for a nanny was soon extended to include cooking and cleaning. The days never ended as the employers found ways to fill the tiniest holes in her busy schedule. With so many people desperate for a job in those days, cheap labour was available and exploitation was common. Yvonne had always had a generous spirit and she did not hesitate to sacrifice all for her family. As time passed, she came to realize that, in Papa's language, she had missed the carefree boat of youth and was in danger of being left stranded on the lonely island of spinsterhood, a very undesirable status in that day.

Yvonne had always had a strong faith in God, but her religious experience often created more questions than answers. While she was single she volunteered several hours a week helping with office work in the vestry of the imposing neighborhood church. One day when she was absorbed in her work, the priest approached her desk, and lifting his long black robe, he clearly revealed his amorous intentions. Shocked and scandalized at the man's nudity, Yvonne fled the scene and ran all the way home. When she told her mother what had happened, she was advised to keep quiet, because if she filed a complaint, it would be her word against his. That was usually the way the religious dirt was swept under the carpet back then. To her horror, it was that same priest who performed her wedding ceremony two years later. It was one more reason Yvonne was so set against the celibacy of priests.

It was in 1934, ten years after their move to the city, that Yvonne met and married my father. In their respective circumstances, it seemed that they were each other's only alternatives. Her life had gone full circle from the farm of her youth to life in Montreal and now to the challenge of a homestead in the back woods. Though money does not buy happiness, at least with some cash, one can be miserable in comfort. In their present circumstances, there was little semblance of comfort; and if our future is fashioned by what we had in our grasp yesterday, she was left to wonder "what future" could possibly emerge from such troubles? The girls watched the evening shadows lengthen over the fields to reach across the valley below. When the sun had set and another summer evening had spread its dusky wings over earth and sky, Yvonne was silent, held captive by many thoughts, which she felt unable to express.

Yvonne's Childhood

Two-year-old Yvonne with brothers, Armand and Oscar, and her parents Delphis and Alma Petit in Ste-Edwidge, 1906.

Yvonne at the convent, 1920.

Nov. 9, 1934.

The Prospect of a Baby

Looking back, it seems to me
That all the grief which had to be,
Left me, when the pain was o'er
Richer than I'd been before. (Anon)

To their joy, Yvonne's seventh pregnancy did not end in a miscarriage. Since she was healthy and strong, she continued her busy life on the farm, all the while preparing for the arrival of the baby. As the months passed, she put on more pounds than anticipated, a problem that would remain with her for years to come. In view of the new arrival, they had built another little house, a temporary dwelling, down the hill near the well. This would provide room for a crib and some of the furniture in storage. It was not a great improvement over the log cabin, but a bigger and better house was always in their plans for the future. It was on October 23, when the first snow fell in 1937 that Yvonne went into labour. Her mother had come to spend a few weeks with her to help her recover and get back on her feet with the new baby. Everyone was confident that things would go well, so it was with no apprehensions that Leo went to fetch the doctor. But for some reason, things did not go well. Observe how soon and to what degree a mother's love begins to operate. Her first provision for her infant is to enter the valley of the shadow of death and deliver its life at the peril of her own. How strong must be the bond that unites their lives!

Many hours into her painful labour, the birth was not progressing, and when at last, Leo returned with the doctor, they realized that he stood to lose his wife. Yvonne gasped to multicolored pain and the world faded away. The doctor, as was common practice in those days, arrived half stoned. He proceeded to anesthetize her and then using forceps, he tried to pull the baby out. That was a far cry from a hospital bed in a bristling nest of machines. Leo was put to work repeatedly pulling Yvonne's heavily sedated body to the foot of the bed by his baby's head. Following many unsuccessful attempts, the doctor looked defeated and told Leo that if the baby did not emerge in the next 15 minutes, he would have to cut him to pieces in order to save the mother's life. At those words, Leo nearly passed out and my grandmother recited every prayer she had ever memorized, in Latin and otherwise. Leo doubled his efforts as he recalled witnessing a complicated calving at his uncle's farm where the veterinarian had proceeded in much the same way. God had mercy on them because, as dawn returned color and life to their isolated homestead, to everyone's relief, a 12-pound baby boy finally emerged. He was exhausted and limp, but he had a bulldog hold on life and hung on. They labeled him Yvon, and he was to become their pride and joy.

When Yvonne finally awoke from that nightmare experience, she felt like she had been pulled through a knothole. She learned about her ordeal and sat for a long time looking down into the face of her son. When she looked up, her eyes had a faraway look as if she saw things beyond the farm kitchen where she sat. What did the future hold for this little child who was just starting out on the long road of his life? Where would he be 20 years from now? She had given birth, had started a life that would never end. Because this child had an eternal soul, she prayed that he would live right and spend his "forever" in heaven. A flood of love washed over her. "Yvon, you are so little and so weak and the way ahead is so long and hard. The world can be such a cruel place, I wish I could always shelter you from harm."

On close examination, she realized that his right arm was limp and lifeless. The paralysis did not go away and would eventually require surgery, but much to their relief, he was not seriously handicapped. As a result of that traumatic experience and their extreme poverty, they decided to have no more babies. During that first pregnancy, Yvonne's body had undergone a metamorphosis. Subtle shifts and expansions of a maternal nature had taken place, her own version of continental drift, but that added dimension of motherhood was a most comfortable fit and she planned to wear it well.

The toddler was boundless energy in perpetual motion. He was very precocious and his parents were convinced that he could do no wrong, as he became an endless source of entertainment for everyone. When Leo laughed at his son's antics, the dog thumped her tail against the wood floor in approval. The family had increased by one and all was well. Without any inhibitions, Yvon talked the ear off anyone who climbed the hill to visit the little family. One day he spotted neighbours walking up the road. "I can speak English", he assured Mama, as he ran to meet them. "Those G D son-of -a-bitch German bastards...." he proudly rattled off. Mama wasn't sure where to hide from embarrassment and contented herself with polite noises, trying to explain that the little one had learned his English with the old veteran, Tom Moon, who lived down the road. Of course, her explanations fell on deaf ears, and the German lady in the group put on a face like a hen's bottom as she promptly settled into a sagging armchair. No amount of back pedaling would diffuse the tension, and poor Yvonne was left to laugh alone when all were gone. She had discovered that there is no way to contain a child's breadth of knowledge, because it is knowledge enriched by ignorance.

When Papa took Yvon to the village for errands, they stopped by the general store to "chew the rag" with the locals. The men kept their hands in their britches pockets and took them out to scratch or to wave them around furiously in an argument. Their talk was mostly "flapdoodle and hogwash", but the laughter was an essential part of rural life. Without it, there might have been fewer survivors. The spittoon was always within reach of the small circle of peasants, but occasionally a little geyser of tobacco juice sizzled on the pot-bellied stove. One fellow had a large protruding stomach, which fascinated the inquisitive three-year-old. "What've you got in there?" he asked.

"Crap," came the crude answer.

"You sure ate a lot of it, didn't you!" retorted Yvon innocently, initiating rounds of laughter from the crowd and a puzzled look on the child.

One day when Yvon expressed curiosity about where people came from, Yvonne explained how God had created Adam and then, his wife Eve from one of Adam's ribs. She tried to add a dusting of logic to their dialogue, not realizing that she was over her head with this boy. Not long after that, her son came running in, holding his side and looking pale. "Is something wrong, Yvon?" to which he replied:

"I have a pain in my side. I think I'm going to have a wife."

The first time that Yvonne took her son to Montreal to visit her relatives, she took a streetcar. The three-year-old bounced to the front to compliment the driver on his fine truck. "Back home," he added, the roads are so bad that Leo can drive only a big army truck."

"Who is Leo?" inquired the driver intrigued.

"He's my papa."

Then he spotted a Catholic priest wearing a long black robe. "Are you a lady or a man?" he asked with a puzzled look on his little face. Yvonne tried to explain quietly that the man was a priest. Still confused, Yvon placed his pudgy little hand on the clergyman's knee and assured him, "You know, Mon Vieux, you would look much better in a nice brown suit like Leo's." Red-faced, Yvonne was relieved to hear the priest burst into uncontrollable laughter.

Because Leo embroidered his speech with religious vocabulary, Yvon had picked up some forbidden words. When they reached her sister's house, Yvonne severely warned Yvon that he was not to use his father's choice vocabulary; "calice" was strictly forbidden here. To her relief, the three-year-old behaved remarkably well, until they were leaving when he piped up in a very clear voice, "I was good, eh Yvonne; I didn't say "calice", not even once." Then she overheard him say to his cousin who also had curly hair, "When your Mama is mad at your Papa, don't let her comb your hair." He had discovered that Yvonne had a rough hand and that with his tight curls it could be particularly painful when she was short of patience.

"If you don't have wrinkles," Mama used to say, "you haven't laughed enough." If that is so, then Yvon must be the cause of a good portion of Mama's creases. Had she taken the trouble to record all of the child's quips, Mama could have written a very funny book. She had discovered that exploring a child's mind is a territory for which parents have never had a road map. It was their first child that introduced my parents to the delightful originality that bubbles from kids, whose logic goes far beyond the tiny brain of an adult. By the time I arrived, I believe they were better prepared. She claimed that we were the wee ones who enlightened the grownups.

When Yvon was almost four, Yvonne discovered that she was pregnant. It was with mixed feelings that she broke the news to Papa. They both loved children, but the idea of raising a family in poverty did not seem right. In the fall of 1941, a major forest fire roared through their woods. Mama grabbed her heavy four-year-old son and ran for safety. Not many days after that exhausting race, she began to feel a strange numbness on the left side of her entire body. Concerned, she made the long trip to Montreal to consult an obstetrician. The doctor examined her and confirmed that she was indeed pregnant, but that a complication had developed; she was carrying twins and one baby had died. The way to proceed was simply to let the pregnancy continue to term when the live baby would be born. In the meantime, the other fetus would remain in the uterus as a benign tumor. He advised her therefore to remain close to the hospital as this was considered a high-risk pregnancy. Of course that would be impossible, so Yvonne had to return home to spend the winter on the farm, hoping that no emergency would occur when all roads might remain closed for weeks. She took extra precautions in order to avoid trouble and to carry her baby to term. In spite of challenging circumstances, she did not lose hope in the dark months when hope was hard to find.

As soon as the roads were manageable in late April, Leo drove her to the train to make sure he did not have to witness another birth at home. He had seen enough of that for a lifetime! Leo kissed her goodbye and Yvonne watched the winding road swallow his truck. With no money, Yvonne felt like a freeloader among her relatives, although it was good to see them all again. When her labor started in mid-May, Yvonne was in the Royal Victoria Hospital with a competent staff. A healthy baby girl was born without complications, and I became the second trophy of those humble folk. I was named

Leola for Papa, just as my brother had been given the masculine form of Mama's name. Within 16 months of my birth, another little girl was born and our family was complete. They named her Lizette and we grew up like twins, inseparable and good buddies to this day. Compared to Yvonne's childhood, three was a small family, but in their circumstances, we made an entirely satisfactory crowd.

Royal Victoria Hospital

Montreal   Dec. 4th. 1941

Mrs. Leo Caya,
La Minerve, Co. Labelle,
Que.

Dear Mrs. Caya:

On Dec. 1st. we visited your friend, Mrs.Bilodeau,
Dorchester St., because we had not heard from you since you
left the hospital. Mrs. Bilodeau tells us that she has written
you advising you to come back, and we want to do the same, as
it is very important for you to have medical care all during
your pregnancy. If you are getting this care at home will you
please let us know. If not, would you please come to clinic
here on Wednesday, Dec. 10th., at two o'clock. This is important
and we hope you will understand.

Sincerely yours,

Miss Christina F, Goodwin
SOCIAL SERVICE DEPARTMENT
WOMEN'S PAVILION

CFG*W

The Prospect of a Baby

Yvon, Mama and baby Leola.

Two-year-old Leola.

Leola and Lizette in 1947.

Three-year-old Yvon
and Puppy.

Leo's logs at the sawmill, 1947.

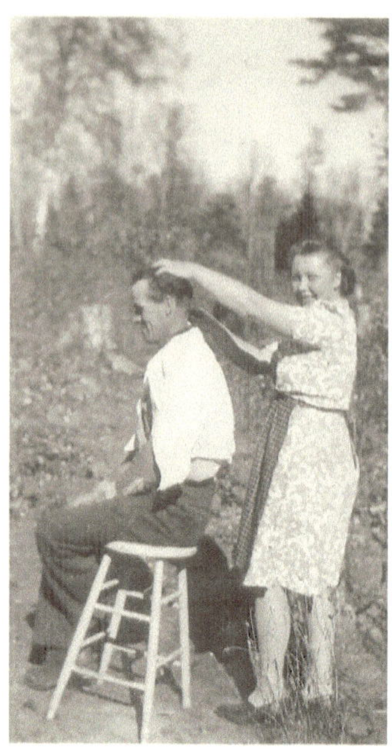

Vally cutting.
Leo's hair, 1946.

Bee and Queen on lot 50.

Leola and Lizette by the
water pump, 1946.

Yvon in hospital, 1945.

School

Life's challenges are not meant to break us,
But to bend us toward God.

The year 1945 marked not only the end of the war, but also the time my brother, now almost eight, should be in school; but here again, Yvonne faced another dilemma. There was no school that far beyond the village. In fact, the nearest little school was almost five miles away over the mountains. Many of the children of Protestant families in our neighborhood had limited schooling because they were expected to walk long distances and there were no resources for them. It seemed a trivial matter for some folks at the time. School buses had not yet been introduced in French rural Quebec, where the one or two-room schoolhouses were built within walking distance for most French Catholic children. No amount of negotiating with the local authorities brought any results, so Mama's only option had been to home school each one of us at an early age.

Lacking all formal teaching materials, Mama taught our inquisitive little minds numbers, letters, colors, shapes, sizes, time, and about trees, flowers, vegetables, berries, farming tools, animals and birds. We found pleasure in the tiniest discovery and pride in every achievement. Like all children, we had the uncanny ability to wash away the dust of dull routine and find excitement in new experiences. She had to be very creative; and to her credit, each one of us learned to read and write before we set foot inside a school. All along our path, Mama taught us to stand tall, walk alone and face the world with confidence. I am convinced that in those circumstances, my mother's heart was our best schoolroom.

With their usual drive, my parents continued to write to every possible source to find a boarding school where we could acquire a proper education. The list of difficulties that lay ahead, not the least of which was the lack of funds, did not speak in their favor. The bureaucracy strangled and stifled any effort on their part to solve this dilemma. For anyone else, the task would have been daunting as most people looked upon the government with its multiple levels of departments in rather the same way as upon the Almighty, invisible and omnipotent; but for Yvonne this only strengthened her resolve to fight for her family. We were her precious trophies, her only real wealth and she would fight tooth and nail on our behalf. The fingers of frustration broke through her normal determination, laying their icy touch on her soul. Would she win this battle?

Finally someone put them in touch with a small protestant home mission that took in children like us who lived in remote areas, to enable them to attend the public school in that village. Because this home did not cater to the rich, the cost of room and board was subsidized by the home missions board of the United Church of Canada and became affordable and accessible to all families in the same predicament.

By the time arrangements could be made, it was January 1946 and my brother was eight years old. He had spent several weeks in Montreal at the children's hospital where he had undergone surgery on his arm to repair the damage received at birth. Words could never adequately describe the pain that broke our hearts when he departed. We all suffered from this separation, but none as profoundly as Yvonne because her firstborn had just been torn from her. When Yvon was tucked in with his brown suitcase, Papa cranked the engine of the old army truck. The big engine coughed and sputtered to life and rattled off down the road. We were left with the dull ticking of the clock, a metronome to our thoughts.

I vividly remember how Mama worked out her grieving in an orgy of house cleaning. My sister and I felt that our big brother had been cut adrift from the bonds of our family. Indeed, the distance that separated us was prohibitive and we would be reunited only at Easter, if the roads were open. That would be the first of many lonely winters for Yvonne as she wondered why, why must she suffer such a painful experience? All those months and years her son would be growing up among strangers, precious years snatched from her.

School

These thoughts tore at the very fabric of her soul. It wasn't fair! But life had never treated her fairly and this last sorrow was only one more in a long list of painful experiences. She had to remind herself in logical terms, that it remained the only option at the time. With her strength of character, I believe that Mama was able to step back and look at the big picture in the tangle of events and troubles and discover the blessings that often wear the disguise of suffering.

Though I was only four, I clearly remember the excitement generated by the occasional brief letter from my brother or the folks in charge of the children's home. We gathered around the oil lamp at the kitchen table to listen as Mama read and reread the same message, as if to discover new details or more information about her son's adjustment to his new surroundings. Was he well treated? Was he lonely? Would he tell her if things did not go well? I shall never forget Yvon's return home after those long weary months. The tears flowed freely as he tried to answer all the questions we rained upon him and we swapped yarns and our dreams of what might have been had we all been together. His home schooling had paid off and he was promoted to grade three in June. By then he spoke fluent English and we were appropriately impressed by his knowledge. Of course he continued to work in the fields with Papa during the summer, but we also found time to go fishing, swimming and whenever possible, he found ways to tease and exasperate his sisters as all brothers do. Every year the summer slipped by much too fast and Labour Day weekend, which marked the time of his leaving, seemed to pounce on us like a rain cloud. Even in childhood, it seemed to me that our lives were filled with goodbyes. I remember Mama leaning against the indifferent porch railing; the tears she had conquered all afternoon poured unheeded down her cheeks. "Why, oh God, do you afflict me so?"

The second year of Yvon's schooling, the approaching Christmas vacation was creating a good deal of excitement around our house as we prepared for his arrival. Mama baked an assortment of goodies in anticipation of her son's homecoming, and Papa talked about having another man around the house. The day before Papa was to make the trip to bring Yvon home at last, the weather changed. A cold, slate-colored miserable day frowned down on our region, as the howling wind threatened to undo all our efforts for a happy Christmas. Papa wondered whether he should try to leave in spite of the approaching storm, knowing that with winter road conditions, the danger of not returning was very real. He and Mama decided that he wait at home until the blizzard had passed. But that was no ordinary snowstorm. It choked up the roads in deep drifts for miles around, isolating entire communities for days. When it was over, Papa was so determined to fetch his son home for Christmas that he began to shovel the road by hand. He worked for hours and covered a distance of nearly two miles with the help of a neighbour, Francis Vetter, but no one else shared his zeal, and the task proved impossible for two men. When more snow began to fall, he had to concede defeat. It was a tearful Christmas for our family that year, as we focused on the empty space at the table and the unopened gift under the tree. That is a memory I would rather forget.

Eight-year-old Yvon,
starting school in Namur, 1946.

The Inferno

One summer the heat became unbearable. It had not rained for weeks and the garden showed signs of despair in spite of our efforts to water. The steady hum of insects intercepted by the sharp chirping of cicadas, accentuated the stillness. Each day the sun shone from a heaven of brass and the heat wave sat heavy on the land. When the sun had reached the zenith and the breezeless torpor of midday lay heavy around us, it seemed that the world was breathing in slow motion, not a cloud in sight. Across the sun-drenched fields and pastures, a dry wind swept in from the south, bringing no relief. The setting sun was a huge angry ball, pulling in its flames over the horizon. As the drought dragged on, our surface well ran dry for the first time, adding to our discomfort. Papa informed us that the land was so parched that the corners of the property were beginning to curl up. He called it the 15-year drought that lasted all summer.

September crept around and Yvon was duly delivered to the boarding home but the weather did not improve. The sun continued to pour forth its angry heat and the torrid air settled over the land like the breath of Hades. Then the inevitable happened. A spark ignited a forest fire. The impending disaster was lurking in the thick underbrush and ready to burst into full fury, when Papa caught sight of the billowing smoke. He was hauling logs at the time and the horses took notice and there was nervous tension in their stride. Racing toward the house, Papa called out orders for Mama to unhitch the team while he went for help. As he ran toward the truck, flames were already licking the dry grassy slope and the north wall of our field was a raging inferno.

He cranked the old truck to a full roar and hoisted me up beside him. I was only about four at the time and it felt like I was peering down from the second storey of a house. The gearshift was a long affair that seemed unpredictable in its travels. I huddled out of its reach every time it came my way.

Not many years ago, I had the hilarious experience of traveling in a primitive bus in Mexico with a similar contraption. It brought back to mind my childhood adventures. Shaking and rattling, as though ready to fall apart, the truck bounded over the rutted lane toward the main road. Our mission was to alert the neighbors along the way and fetch fire-fighting equipment in the village, seven miles off. By the time we had located the necessary hoses and pumps and completed the fourteen-mile round trip, the community had mobilized with shovels, rakes and all manner of weapons and when the wind shifted, they had managed to extinguish the flames. It was nothing short of a miracle and although our efforts proved redundant, Papa was extremely grateful for the timely help. Things could have been much worse, but the landscape to the north had changed. Tall balsams and spruce that had once stood majestic in their glory, were reduced to blackened, witch-like skeletons. That fire was not the first, nor would it be the last to threaten our property over the years. Living beyond the reach of any type of fire brigade left the homesteaders vulnerable to such calamities.

The Boarding Home

When tomorrow comes and life beats against
your safe haven;
Remember the power of honest pain and blended
tears.
Braving pain is often the only way to reach a new
shoreline.

It was 1949 when my sister, Lizette, and I would join my brother in the same boarding home in Namur, a small village between Montebello and St-Jovite. At six and seven years old respectively, we were leaving behind an empty nest, Mama's greatest pain. The sky seemed to be a weary shade of gray when we stole a last look at our little house on the hillside. It would be Christmas when we returned. As the old car rattled along, we all relapsed into hurt silence. We knew that our parents would be returning home with heavy hearts and little more than broken dreams. They were sacrificing their lives to give us the best they could afford. We had grown to understand that sorrow was the stuff of their lives and we were about to share a good portion of it ourselves. When we said goodbye, Mama's face was a study in sorrow. Her heart was wrapped up in her three children, and she was leaving them behind. On the verge of tears, she scanned the horizon to get her thoughts on safer ground. Papa was putting up a brave front, but he was unable to speak, and simply held us in a warm embrace. Like many pioneers, they were giving of themselves that others should reap the benefits.

We were duly handed over to the matron in charge of the home. She was a well-upholstered lady in her fifties with gray hair rolled up Amish fashion. Judging from her appearance, I guessed that she was a no-nonsense person expecting good behavior. Her husband Abraham, 20 years her senior, was the minister of the little French Protestant parish of Namur, one of only two villages in the province without a Catholic church. It had been with some hesitation that my parents had settled on this option for our schooling because they were Roman Catholic, as were most French-speaking families in Quebec at that time. Religion had always been a mystery that no one had ever felt much desire to stir. For most people, Christianity was only skin-deep, yet they clung with undying fidelity to the superstitions and traditions that had been handed down and preserved with a tenacity that ignorance had failed to shake. To so much as question the religious teaching of the church was a heresy; so it took considerable courage and daring for my parents to step out of line and send their children to a Protestant institution. The change of allegiance was not just a threat to an entrenched custom, but also a challenge to their distinctness and identity as a people. The Roman Catholic religion was part of the culture of French Canadians at that time. Of course Papa's chief motivation was to provide us with the basic education, which the local authorities had denied us back home. In addition, we had the bonus of learning in an English environment. It was ultimately this attraction that proved stronger than their ties to the Roman Catholic Church, a very unusual step in that day.

Their decision put them squarely in the wrong court and initiated a long period of persecution when they were labeled "communists" and accused of heresy and subversion. They were not merely fighting a dictatorial regime, but sowing seeds of freedom, and all the while, we were receiving a bilingual education, which proved to be an invaluable asset that would eventually bring relief to our troubled future. For our family this marked the beginning of a long spiritual journey. My parents were persuaded that the Holy Bible held the answers to many of their questions about religion, and before long that book found its way to our house and into our hearts.

How does a six or seven-year-old child react when left among strangers? It is such a brutal and devastating trauma that I can compare it only to an abortion. I still remember Mama with two fat tears coursing down her cheeks. She tried to be strong but this was too painful. Her babies had all been snatched from her, and she would be compelled to face her tomorrows alone. Lizette and I wept uncontrollably, finding little comfort in each other's presence. After a long while, our matron became annoyed and, with her mouth buttoned into its most disapproving line, she ordered us to stop the blubbering and to settle down. We did our best to keep our whimpering under control and to be obedient, as Mama had instructed us so often. But the tears were never far from the surface, and ready to overflow at the tiniest provocation. We had to cope with a situation too big even for adults. When the moon came to look in the window on her nightly rounds, she often saw two little faces, wet with tears, lying on the same pillow in that little room off the balcony.

When I look back to the years I spent in that institution, I recall, not only the building, but also the fascinating tales that lie embedded in its walls, for it was more than a building, it was a story in wood and stone. We were assigned a room to ourselves, a luxury we had never had before. The sun was setting and the light filtering through the thick foliage of the old maple tree, gave a curious under-water effect to the room as the shadows wavered against the walls. We could hear the excited voices of the other children down the hall as we sat on the edge of our beds, our legs dangling, with our boxes of clothes propped up beside us. The old-fashioned lace curtains in our bedroom windows played and flirted with the afternoon breeze. A couple of older girls were assigned to help us unpack, and then to show us around the building. As we watched them hang our dresses in the little closet, my sister clung to her old doll with most of its hair loved off. This brought her a measure of comfort in these strange surroundings. When the girls left, Lizette began to cry and I pulled her out to the balcony so we could both cry.

Downstairs was the dining hall with long tables lined with benches for seating some 40 people. The walls were a subdued shade of yellow with several tall windows along the wall opposite the kitchen. The sunlight was fractured by curtains in the open windows creating dancing patterns of light across those long tables. At the far end was the living room, which was more formal. It contained some ancient furniture and a concert piano that was mahogany and full of years. I had never seen such a large instrument before. It seemed to dwarf the room. And right before my eyes was a real fireplace not unlike the pictures I had seen on Christmas cards. I turned to my sister and suggested that perhaps Santa would appear when the snow came. Two large paintings dominated the wall above the chesterfield; one of a kind-looking man surrounded by children and the other of a shepherd and a whole flock of sheep. Over the mantle hung another picture, but it frightened me because it depicted a storm-tossed sail-boat on rough waters. I had always been afraid of storms and deep water, so I preferred the other two pictures.

Before long, a little knot of people entered the room. Among them was Yvon who was engaged in lively conversation with his friends. But even his presence did not offer much comfort at that moment, because the strangeness of the surroundings was just simply overwhelming. The whole building contained so many rooms! To a child, it seemed less like a house than a city. On weekends it would become a maze of long corridors, empty rooms, attics to explore in solitude, a collection of strange noises and smells. When the supper bell rang, youngsters poured in, and the dining hall was soon wedged full of people. The growing crowd of new arrivals sorted themselves onto the long benches along the tables. There was a pause to offer thanks for the food when the silence sliced through the noise like a knife. Everyone sat down and we were served chicken soup, though I'm not certain that a chicken had ever passed through it. With a lump in my throat and a hundred pair of eyes on me, I faced the dilemma of swallowing that meal. I recall how difficult it was to be polite and obedient, all the while trying to stomach a meal with no appetite for food. Every bite seemed to catch in my throat making me gag, not that the food was bad, but I was simply overcome by emotions.

There we met Una, chief cook and bottle washer, whose face gleamed like a polished apple, so tight and shiny in her well-scrubbed skin. She wore a warm, friendly smile that was most reassuring, like a little bit of home away from home.

The Boarding Home

Somehow her simple kindness made the worries of the day seem trivial. On many Sundays to come, when most children went to their respective homes, she would hoist my six-year-old sister onto her lap in the large rocker, and in motherly fashion, comfort a lonely little girl. I know that when I die, Una will find her name written on my heart.

Over the years, I have learned that there are two types of education; one teaches us how to earn a living, the other teaches us how to live. My initial eight years away from home at the school of emotional hard knocks was definitely the latter. Through thick and thin, I learned to relate to all kinds of people; and in the process, I developed a compassion for the underdog, the oddball, the socially inept and other lonely people. Another effect of this experience was the strong bond that developed between my sister and me, as we felt united before a common foe, which was simply a sense of insecurity. I understand now that shared adversity will cement the bonds of friendship. At first the days seemed long and dark like winter days, but it was only September.

One anecdote comes to mind when I recall my first weeks in an English school. This was still a foreign language to us, so we tried to look smart by pretending to understand the instructions. Had the poor teacher only known how clueless we were, she might have been amused. One day she thoroughly explained the procedure for a fire drill and specifically asked if we had understood. Of course we nodded, and when the bell rang, we grabbed our books and headed towards the residence next door. When we looked back and saw everyone lined up outside, we sheepishly returned looking appropriately confused. How awkward to never quite understand the expectations! Language learning presented some confusing guess work, creating surprised looks and occasional outbursts of laughter, telling us it was time to backtrack and try another guess. Day by day, we enlarged our vocabulary and eventually we began to penetrate into the inner sanctum of abstract expressions of the king's lingo. Before many weeks had passed, Mama's home schooling paid off, and I was promoted to grade two with the other seven-year-olds. We had lost our initial fear. Our misgivings had faded as we gained a degree of confidence in our new surroundings. We were learning the language, making friends and time passed with bewildering speed; while for Mama, back at the homestead, the days dragged by in the loneliness of an empty house.

At seven o'clock every morning, the good lady in charge of the home walked up and down the corridors ringing a little bell. It was the wake-up call, which I considered sheer cruelty. I would throw back the covers and kick a warm foot out into the cold world; which was followed by a reluctant companion. Then I would sit on the edge of the bed and stare at the back of my eyelids. Another day was beginning in the framework of our institution, another very predictable day. The girls used a long white enamel sink lined with half a dozen taps with running cold water. (Hot water was reserved for Saturdays when we took turns in the bathtubs.) This was sure to wake us up before we put on our school clothes. New clothes we kept for Sundays when we were scrubbed and polished, because they were too good to be comfortable. Then we went down for breakfast, which consisted of a bowl of hot or cold cereal with milk and toast. The food was good, but I was seldom hungry at that time and found it very hard to swallow even a small portion. Consequently, I looked upon breakfast as a form of punishment.

This was followed by our morning chores, which included washing dishes, making our beds, tidying up our rooms, cleaning sinks, toilets, baths, or sweeping the floors according to our schedules. With little enthusiasm, we generally took turns washing dishes and peeling potatoes as well as various other jobs which children can handle without causing too much damage. Then we brushed our teeth, collected our books, and dressed for school, which was next door. We ran across for lunch and usually played outside before supper. In the evening, all the children sat around the cleared tables with the usual muted racket that filled the study hall to complete homework assignments. We helped each other when necessary and at 8 o'clock we gathered in the living room for evening devotions with our matron, who played the piano and led the singing of songs and hymns. We were usually treated to a bible story and perhaps a quiz on Friday evenings when we were allowed to stay up a little later. Those evenings brought a warm cozy feeling to the close of each day, as in her motherly way, our matron was showing the children that she cared. In spite of her demanding schedule, she came upstairs to make sure we were all tucked in for the night. She knew how much we craved those cuddles, as she became a captive audience for our little concerns and occasional bouts of homesickness. And these rituals were repeated every day and every week, season after season. It was the way of life in a boarding home.

The boarding home next to
St. Paul's United Church, Namur.

Church

Beneath his watchful eye
His saints securely dwell;
That hand which bears all nature up
Shall guard His children well. (Doddridge)

It was in that context that we were introduced to church. Religion had never been part of our lives before. In fact, I didn't know whether we were Catholic or Protestant. The little village church was a typical wooden structure next to the children's home. It was a building that had witnessed all the spiritual tremors of these villagers for at least three generations, judging from the tombstones in the adjacent cemetery. The tall steeple dominating the roof housed a large brass bell, which was rung by pulling a rope in the balcony. The white building was blessed with stained glass windows; a row of tall, narrow windows lining both sides of the chapel and a beautiful round window that shone like an exquisite flower behind the pulpit. There were no plush seats of deep maroon comfort, and the discomfort of the wooden benches, I concluded, was intentional to keep the worshippers from falling asleep. At the front and to the right stood an old harmonium, which we called a melodium. That was a far cry from the magnificent sound from the throat of a pipe organ. When the organist worked it, it sounded pretty colicky, an appropriate match for the tired hymns.

When the reverend, with his snow-white hair, stood up to preach, he reminded me of an antique waiter I had seen in a magazine. His sermons sounded persuasive enough, because what he lacked in content, he made up for in volume. As he uttered long, eloquent prayers couched in lofty theological phrases, it sounded to me as if he were exploring the universe of doctrine and scraping the milky way with big words. It quickly became apparent that my attention span would be no match for their length. My mind usually wandered in a daydream, until a penetrating bellow caught me off guard and pounced on me like a mountain lion. That was my call to attention. The dear man was trying to keep his people focused on eternity while they were racing through time in their respective circles. Though a minister's job is to comfort the afflicted, I am convinced that there were moments when our aging pastor found it necessary to afflict the comfortable. Parishioners were moved to search their souls for cobwebs that must be swept clean.

I shall never forget the first time my sister and I were ushered into that white building for an evening service. We had not yet recovered from the initial shock of leaving home and the tears were still very close to the surface. The September sun filtered through the amber colored glass, creating a melancholic effect I had never before experienced. Perhaps the sound of the pump organ contributed to the sadness, but on that wooden bench, two small girls held hands and wept like little lost sheep. I remember the sleepy head of my sister cradled against my shoulder as I bravely dried her tears. I must have considered that sad experience a necessary evil, which was to be part and parcel of our new lifestyle. It was not a promising start to our religious education.

That little church, the heartbeat of the village, did not falter for local sickness or bad weather. It maintained its quiet rhythm as centerpiece of social life for the community. Christenings and weddings were celebrated, and time and again the earth would be opened up to receive a new burden from that small village. When we attended church in those days, "sin" was still part of the vocabulary. Nowadays, the term "sin" may be deemed "politically incorrect" and even considered offensive.

On succeeding Sundays, we began to enjoy looking around and observing the worshippers as they took their places in the swelling crowd. Because the rectory occupied the front section of the boarding home, we would soon become well acquainted with many of these parishioners. Most of the women were either approaching or well engaged in middle age and were very involved in the church, organizing bazaars and other social events. In fact, the church was the hub of most village activities. These ladies could cook up a storm and whip together a feast like magic, as they clucked over their grains of gossip. Secrets were hushed about behind closed doors from stove to sink and back again. A little eavesdropping could provide much amusement, and sometimes one seed well planted might produce a harvest of embellished tales. Of course these dear ladies were not mean-spirited or spiteful, only in need of a little excitement in their lives. While their tongues moved as fast as their hands, we caught occasional funny lines that sent us into fits of laughter.

"My son's too fussy about girls. Looks like I'll end up havin' to find 'im a wife and be draggin' 'im off to the preacher myself. And don't you go making funnies about that. It ain't his fault he's shy with girls."

Some of these women worked at the boarding home in various capacities and they became part of our lives. Although they were all different, each was special and I have fond memories of every one. One dear lady came to the home every Monday to help with the laundry. She was a portly woman, well past her prime, who steered her body around obstacles with remarkable ease. Her face was made for tenderness, but life had disciplined it. She may have been suffering from arthritis, as I recall her frequent complaints of a pain in her upper left cutlet. With her nasal voice, she sometimes sounded like she was about to be ushered into the divine presence, but I especially remember her kindness to me when I was recovering from a tonsillectomy so far from home.

There was another helper who showed up every Friday to change the beds and tidy the rooms. She was very efficient, and more than once her devastating broom played havoc with my collection of paper dolls. English was a second language for her, and I recall the time she declined an invitation because she was "decomposed" on account of a misfortune. The night before she had broken the "fonygraph" she treasured. Though her task was not overwhelming, she wore her troubles and old grievances about her like a shroud. I concluded that her troubles had crawled deep into her bones and remained anchored in the depths of her soul. Life was a struggle for many folks in the early 50's and that dear lady was no exception. Apparently, she had a son who had suffered a nervous breakdown. Some time ago, I learned that he had crossed the line and taken up residence in the comforting country of the deranged. So many years later, it is not without compassion that I remember that kind mother.

Beatrice, bless her heart, worked in the kitchen and always brought with her a warm smile, and a happy manner like a bushel of sunshine. She was Una's younger sister, from a family of some 15 children and somehow managed to see the bright side of every situation. No matter what happened, it seemed that our sunshiny Beatrice came right side up laughing. Her cheerful disposition proved to be the best weapon against the gloom that could settle over our lives on dull days. Such people, I am convinced, are capable of riding over the rough roads of life without noticing the bumps. The last time I saw her, which was not many years ago, her attitude had not changed. I can only thank God for the fond memories I have of her.

Our head mistress had a big heart and plenty of compassion to spread around, but the responsibilities were endless, and her strength was not always equal to the task. She was strict and relied on her tongue as an instrument of discipline. When she delegated tasks, though she couched it in a polite tone, it was still a demand. She had to supervise, not only the hired help, but also our assigned chores to maintain the smooth operation of the "home". I remember peeling potatoes in the cellar. This was a dark space next to a smaller room full of preserves and dominated by a large barrel of molasses. For a serious offence, one could be banished to the cellar for a period of time. The culprit always hoped, as night fell, that he would not be forgotten in the "belly of the beast".

I have a fond memory of our matron trying to coax my seven-year-old sister from the top branch of a huge pine tree by the schoolyard. I wondered why she was offering Lizette candy to persuade her to come down "right away". When she had succeeded in getting her to return to ground level, that dear lady made very clear her legitimate concern about tree climbing, and in no uncertain terms! Lizette had obviously not figured out that her stunt had pushed our matron's blood pressure over the limit that day; but she did not repeat that exploit again, at least not in her presence.

The boarding home next to St. Paul's United Church, Namur.

School

Study and learn before you grow old,
Learning is better than silver and gold;
Silver and gold will vanish away.
But a good education will never decay.

A mountain dominated the small cluster of buildings that nestled at its feet, the church, the community hall, the boarding home, the rectory and the school. The school was a two-storey wooden structure, which housed four classrooms, each with multiple grades. It boasted central heating with a wood-burning furnace in the basement. The janitor, Mr. Welburn, was a kind old gentleman from the village, who also kept the fire going all winter. I remember the day my teacher called on him to bring a large block of firewood into the classroom. She was determined to teach one boy a lesson. He had the nasty habit of chewing on his pencil, so the teacher insisted that he chew on that monstrous piece of wood like a beaver until he was satisfied. I doubt that the strategy worked, but it was funny. That teacher had yet to learn that the human mind can absorb only what the human seat can endure.

Being a rural school in a remote community, it was difficult to recruit qualified staff. It followed that the school board sometimes employed high school graduates as teachers. These young people usually worked one or two years before moving on. Somehow, experienced or not, our teachers managed to impress us with their learning, and we progressed, because they had set aside distance and time to touch us with their lives. I have since learned that until a student knows how much you care, he won't care how much you know. Somehow those fine people helped shape us kids into the responsible adults we eventually became.

With a classroom full of rapscallions, our teachers' original starch was a mite wilted by the end of the first week, but once we had them broken in, they made great strides. I recall one young man who inspired me to love geography. He had a way of dramatizing and painting such humorous pictures in his lessons that we learned in spite of the limited resources available in those days. One such lesson might go like this, as he described the vast expanse of the grasslands on the Canadian Prairies. "And don't even think of climbing a tree! Out there, a woodpecker has to pack a box lunch. So flat, a gopher has to kneel to eat dinner."

"How did they heat their stoves?"

"They used 'bois de vache' (which, it turned out, was buffalo dung, also known as prairie wood.)"

I still remember studying the map of Europe with such lines as, "Russia got Hungary and fried Turkey in Greece" and " When China sticks her dragon snout into the ribs of the Russian bear; when snout tickles ribs, the result is not a chuckle from the bear, but a growl and perhaps a slap of the paw...", meaning the threat of war. I learned that writing a story in the first person did not mean writing it as Adam would. His sense of humor generally got the point across, and everyone caught the drift.

One teacher's way of looking displeased impressed her will upon her students without the necessity of words. Her eyes spoke volumes when her brow lowered and her lips tightened. Another young lady, fresh out of high school discovered that teaching had its minefields, like the day I innocently asked her what circumcision meant in the middle of a lesson. When her face turned crimson, I figured I should not have asked. That is probably when I discovered the importance of a dictionary. So went the lessons about our vast country, half a world away from our little village in the mountains. We learned, and that little school produced many bilingual people, who went on to successful careers in business or continued their studies in college and university. Education was a serious matter for these families, and I was privileged to be part of that small community half a century ago.

In the summer of 2003, there was a school reunion in Namur, the first one in the history of that village. Through

School

laughter and tears, the weekend was spent catching up with folks we had not seen in decades, among them several of my elementary school teachers. Many young people commented on the strong bonds that still linked the older generation to that small village. We had been such a tightly knit community for many years that we simply picked up where we had left off. I had the awesome privilege of addressing that large assembly and sharing some amusing anecdotes of many years ago.

Come December, the whole school, perhaps 100 children from grades one through ten, engaged in preparing the Christmas concert, an annual event and highlight of the year for the school. The Christmas pageant mirrored the hearts of these villagers. The performances included songs, drama, and music. As we rehearsed for that special evening, the school was transformed into a din of merry chaos. Small children, noisy and exuberant, seemed to bounce off the walls. At times our teachers must have felt like members of the British House of Lords, with a certain ceremonial air, but no one to pay attention to anything they said. I have since learned that the only things children can wear out faster than shoes or the seat of their pants, are parents and teachers. These activities, however, gave us a sense of belonging. Teachers and students developed a special bond of friendship as we rehearsed and decorated the community hall together.

We children spent the mornings attempting to finish our lessons and devoted the afternoons to rehearsing our various lines for the plays, everyone hurrying about with great purpose. Smack in the middle of rehearsals, our teacher caught a nasty cold. Then her cold fell from her nose to her lungs and with incessant coughing, her voice fell below zero, a full octave below her normal squeak. This added a new dimension to the fun of rehearsing and, I suspect that our behavior might have contributed to her condition. At last, before our eyes stood the bedecked tree, festooned with all manner of strings and baubles. The magic of it! With the parish hall glittering in unaccustomed splendor, there was a sense of anticipation in the air. The world would never be the same again.

It was on the last day of school that first year that I heard the tinkling of sleigh bells. Down the road from the direction of the village trotted a team of horses, pulling a red sleigh piled high with Christmas presents; and holding the reins, sat Santa Claus himself. I can almost feel my pounding heart, as I clearly remember running for my sister and shouting, "Come quickly! I just saw the real Santa Claus drive by in his sleigh full of presents, but he didn't stop! Do you suppose he will come back?"

That evening, at the concert, our class had just covered itself with glory and we sat fascinated by the older children's performance. The parish was extremely privileged to have Miss Aline Favier, a gifted musician and a strong artistic presence in our midst. She was an ornament to her profession, and in a few short weeks, she had polished a crowd of rough stones into lovely gems that graced the concert hall that evening. Once again, with the entire population present, the pageant was an outstanding success.

When all had been said and done, and the applause had died down, the sound of sleigh bells was heard outside and everyone turned around. As the doors opened, Santa appeared at the back of the hall through a cloud of frosty air with a red face and a bag full of presents. I was so excited that I was not sure whether to laugh or cry. The jolly round fellow ho!ho!ho!'ed his way to the front of the packed hall, where he adjusted his specs and began to read the names on those packages. We children held our collective breath, hoping that we had not been forgotten in so large a crowd and such a mountain of gifts. At last, my sister's name was called, and I knew that we were included in Santa's list. I cannot recall what we received, for that was not the important thing. It was the excitement of being part of that special event that has remained with me all these years.

When it was all over, we were shepherded back to our lodgings where cups of hot chocolate greeted us. It was long past our bedtime, when I saw the hands of the clock closing like scissor blades on midnight, snipping off another day, and what a day it had been! It had marked the end of our first semester in school and away from home, a slow and winding path through time. When we were tucked into bed that night, we were too exhausted to remember that the next morning would bring the best present of all, the long-awaited trip back to the homestead after four long months away from home.

Namur Intermediate School, 1950s.

Emily Gouin and her husband the Rev. Abraham Gouin
with some of the children in the boarding home, Teddy
Vetter, Peter Hall, Lizette, Leola, Danny V., Hazel V., Rosie V.
(Back row) Emily V., Alice V., Kathleen V.,
Rolland Auchon, 1952.

Lizette, Yvon and Leola,
on my birthday,
Namur, 1951

Yvon with Papa,
Namur, 1951.

Home for Christmas

There is magic in the simple things...
In all this wondrous season brings.

The following morning heralded the day we had anticipated for four long months. The three of us piled into an ancient car that rattled off and slowly headed north along the narrow, snow-covered roads. After what seemed like many hours, the car nosed its way around the last bend in the narrow lane that led to the post office of our own village. There stood Papa's team of horses, gray Clydesdales with white feet that reminded me of majorette boots. Papa had come to meet us! Laughter and tears mingled as we embraced and settled in the sleigh with our old suitcases. We were nearing home. Another seven miles and we would see our dear mama at last. To this day, the sound of sleigh bells and the odour of horses conjures up my whole childhood.

It felt like the cold wind had pushed the edge of daylight into dusk by the time the horses climbed the last steep hill, and we spotted the light glowing in the window of our house. Standing on the hillside, the little cottage faced the teeth of the east wind. In fact, its vulnerable position exposed it to the four winds. The wood stove, consequently, was the very heartbeat of the building, and dominated the first floor that served as kitchen, dining room and living room.

We could not tumble out of the sleigh fast enough it seemed, as we raced for the house. Mama's open arms engulfed all three of us at once, and another flood of tears vied with laughter, as words tumbled out and got into one another's way. Mama had always managed to hold our family close together by enfolding us in her own warm spirit. That day will remain etched in my memory as one of the highlights of that first year of our education.

Supper was ready and the aroma of home cooking was

like sweet music. I sniffed luxuriously as we instinctively set-tled into our respective chairs to enjoy good food and try to catch up on four months of absence. Before many hours had passed, the warmth of the stove and the dim light of the oil lamp conspired to make bedtime most appealing. Upstairs in the loft, the moon had just risen to such a height as to pour into our window, painting a box of daylight on the floor. With that bright shaft of light, we could have dispensed with the oil lamp altogether as we quickly disappeared beneath the waves of the heavy quilts to sleep soundly in the security of home.

All night the east wind blew bitterly, as though chipped off an iceberg and, by the next morning, the leaden sky turned darker and darker as it crept lower. Then the blizzard set in. We knew that the storm would only intensify before the day was over. By midday, the wind was not just noise, but push and shove. The fire roaring in the stove kept the house toasty warm, while the blizzard, like a thick cloak, cocooned the kitchen in velvet darkness. Of course, we did not mind the gloom, because of our joy at being safely tucked in with our parents.

Outside, nothing moved but the wind and the snow. As the hours ticked by, the snow piled up, inching its way to-wards the windows. Papa looked concerned as he puffed on a succession of cigarettes. He knew that it might take up to two weeks before the roads would be opened again even for the horses to travel. That was the least of our worries, as we secretly hoped to prolong our ten-day visit and delay the inevitable good-byes. But for a logger who earns his liv-ing felling trees and hauling logs, a heavy snowfall can be a nightmare. Our concern was for a more immediate problem. Would Santa make it to our house on such a night?

Papa had to leave the comfort of the house and battle the snowdrifts to feed the horses in the barn and fetch water at the well. Thawing and priming the water pump outside in winter was always a challenge, but carrying those heavy pails through the deep snow was a daunting task. The rea-son we did not have indoor plumbing was that the bedrock had to be blasted with dynamite, and Papa was repeatedly denied the necessary permit. It had been one of the many lost battles in his war with the local authorities.

By evening, the wind was subsiding, but the night and the storm between them had sealed off the world. The next morning the storm had spent itself, leaving in its wake a world muffled and soft in white eiderdown.. When the sun rose and stretched over the hill, it spread a rainbow of color over the snowdrifts. It was so exciting to try our old toboggan again on the steep familiar slopes. The snow was deep and our legs were short, a combination that rapidly sapped every ounce of energy, and before many hours had passed, we were exhausted and chilled to the bone. We lumbered back to the house, where we knew that Mama had hot bread and molasses ready for us. Our wet mittens and boots would find their way to the stove to dry. That was the clothes dryer of the day in every home.

In the meantime, Yvon had gone into the woods to help Papa choose a Christmas tree. They struggled through the deep snow and returned with a modest little balsam, which was parked in the corner of the kitchen farthest from the stove and left to melt its load of snow. In the evening, we proceeded to decorate its branches with the few familiar glass balls, tinsel and paper ornaments which Mama had stored away in the abandoned chicken coop or some other secret corner. The wonderful aroma of fresh balsam filled the room as the warm air thawed the branches. With the oil lamp reflected in the shiny balls, the evergreen carried a fragrance full of memories of past Christmases, of happy times and surprises. Before we knew it, another day had slipped by, another precious day of a special week. More hugs and cuddles, and we were off to bed again, this time with a sense of anticipation.

The sun had not yet returned from its trip around the world when I awoke to a familiar sound. I could hear the faint scratching of a match, then the soft light from the oil lamp flooded the stairway and Papa's shadow danced grotesquely on the wall as he moved about the kitchen lighting the fire. I whispered to my sister that it was Christmas. Perhaps Santa had come. "Do you suppose that the storm might have kept him away?" she managed, still half asleep. At that we both jumped out of bed onto the icy floor and peeped downstairs at the Christmas tree. We both shrieked with laughter at the sight of wrapped presents. The old boy had come through the storm after all! Those very modest gifts were more precious to us than gold, for they contributed to add that Christmas to my collection of warm memories, another genuine expression of love. For many hours we brooded joyfully over our small collection of presents that seemed so magnificent to us.

After a breakfast of pancakes and homemade jam, the lagging daylight asserted itself and I remember clearly taking in all the details of the intricate designs on the frosted single pane windows. The day unfolded, excitement spilling over into every corner. We spent that day playing with our new paper dolls and coloring books in the warm kitchen, listening to Christmas music on the battery-operated radio. Mama had fetched potatoes and carrots from the cellar and, before we knew it, dinner was on the table and it was like old times again. In lieu of a turkey, a fat chicken lay in state, the perfect Christmas dinner.

As I look over my spacious kitchen with its timesaving appliances, I think back to that little kitchen on the homestead. It wasn't filled with gadgets. It didn't even have running water, only two buckets of cold water and a dipper on the counter, but it was bursting with cheer. Sunlight always seemed to stream in through the windows onto the painted wood floor, making the room bright and cozy. Narrow frilly curtains framed the windows and added a feminine touch to the simple room. The old wooden table was where we ate our meals and then played cards, checkers, or browsed through Eaton's catalogue. There was always a kettle purring on the stove along with a pot of stew or bread baking in the oven. I loved the aroma of molasses cookies or apple pies.

Returning from morning chores was such a treat. It might be still dark outside, but inside the kitchen, there was the soft glow of the oil lamp until daylight asserted itself. The table was soon covered with piles of hot pancakes and molasses, or bacon and eggs sizzled in the background. Cholesterol was unknown in those days. Today we have engineered

Home for Christmas

movement out of our lives, but back then we worked hard, played hard, got hungry and gratefully ate whatever the Lord provided. I remember Mama's chicken and rice soup seasoned with celery or parsley and served with hot bread and fresh butter. We slurped through soup heaven when we came in from the cold. Such simple fare still triggers warm memories of my childhood. So many years later, winter carries memories of a warm fire, hot soup, heavy blankets and frosted windows.

Three days after Christmas, we heard the jingling of bells outside and, much to our delight, two teams of horses appeared at the top of the hill, pulling a huge wooden roller. The roller was filled with sand and simply flattened the snow, making the road surface hard enough for horses and sleighs. That was the method used before the days of the snowplow. Our road had been opened in record time. It would be possible for us to visit an old couple who lived alone about two miles away. The sleigh was not only practical in cold weather, but much more in keeping with Christmas. We burrowed under heavy buffalo rugs and watched the stars on a clear velvet sky, as the runners squeaked over the crisp hard snow. The days marched by. December was torn from the general store calendar by the stove, bringing the year and the decade to an end.

> Lord, I'm standing at the door
> Of this new untarnished year;
> Help me to be all that I should be
> To those that I hold dear.

Every New Year's Day, when he returned from the barn at daybreak, Papa turned on the radio. The sound of traditional reels and lively folk songs filled the house as he tap-danced around the kitchen whistling a rollicking tune. Maybe the new calendar held a promise of better days ahead, because Papa was always in a jovial mood as he greeted the family with the words: "Bonne et heureuse annee!" and Mama sang some of Grandpapa's old songs from her youth.

"C'est aujourd'hui le premier jour de l'an;
Il faut le feter en chantant... »
We seldom went anywhere, but we all tried to be upbeat as we ushered in the New Year. We spent the afternoon around the table playing cards or checkers and each told stories that seemed to outdo the previous one. Then Mama would turn to Papa with, "Leo, you remember when..." and he would be off again. The signs of stress on their faces seemed to fade in those happy moments. Soon the sun sent the shadow of the barn stealing across the field and Mama was preparing supper. It was late afternoon and the day was already growing old, when Papa lit the Coleman lamp for us and left for the barn with a lantern. In the darkness of a northern winter the days are too short. As we set the table, we cast strange shadows on the walls and were startled by the occasional glimpse of our own reflection in the darkened windows.

The holidays passed in a flurry of sledding, shrieks of laughter, wet mittens, cold feet, and red cheeks. Before we knew it, two weeks had gone by and we were packing again. Though we were more than ready to graduate after that first semester, we knew that many years of expatriation yawned before us. The grief of leaving home is among the memories that I could willingly dispense with. We all felt like some of the gray had left the sky and entered our hearts as we realized that another succession of endless weeks would separate us from our next reunion, probably at Easter.

Papa seemed to procrastinate as he hitched the horses to the sleigh and secured our luggage. Mama placed hot bricks at our feet under the heavy buffalo furs that covered everything but our eyes. It was bitterly cold and dangerous for frostbite. But what really bothered everyone was saying goodbye again. The repeated agony of separation was devastating enough, but remembering the empty room and Mama's brave face as she held back the tears, and knowing that in a moment all the sorrow of her isolation would be upon her was heartbreaking. After our departure, I knew that the silence would be with her again, all the louder. I could picture her sitting by the window facing the valley, overwhelmed with sadness.

Home for Christmas

Once we reached the snow-cleared road, the horses were left in a shelter and we faced the challenge of starting the old Chrysler that had been parked in the same spot for several weeks. Those were the days when most vehicles ran on a hope and a prayer. That jalopy ran on faith and rattles. Starting the engine in winter proved to be a recurring battle of wills, but Papa was an obstinate man and usually found a way to persuade the stubborn machine to submit. That day was no exception as he laboured over the engine with the energy of desperation. Finally, with the engine roaring, we set off to cover the remaining 65 miles of icy roads over the mountains from village to village, sometimes tossing us about like watermelons in a wheelbarrow. The roar of the engine drowned out our anguished protests from the back seat. When at last the car came to an abrupt stop and the engine was turned off, we were upended and dusted off, no worse for wear, but another goodbye stood before us. Papa had to go back home. It always left an empty feeling in the pit of the stomach.

Winter at School

In early January in that part of the world, the days are short with dusk falling around four o'clock. It was a challenge for us to remain seated and focused from 9 a.m. to 4 p.m., considering that in the freedom of the homestead, we had been in perpetual motion. We ran across the yard to the home next door for lunch and played outside at all recess breaks. However, with homework and our assigned chores, the days passed remarkably fast. On Saturdays, the children who did not go home for the weekend gathered at a little hill behind the boarding home with sleds, toboggans, pieces of cardboard, or even the seat of the pants to slide for hours. By the end of the day we reluctantly returned for supper, red-cheeked and exhausted

Sunday afternoons were spent at the village rink, fascinated by our hockey heroes who were competing with neighboring teams. Before many weeks had passed, we dug out men's old hockey skates from the attic and laced them up over our shoes. Our first attempts were pathetic, but we soon learned to stand up on the blades and then actually move around. I felt like a real hero as I proudly wobbled around the rink on those ancient blades. My sister was always more reckless and, by far the better athlete, so she quickly mastered the skill and could handle a hockey stick with ease. Before long she was giving the boys a rough time on the ice. In fact, her ease of adjustment put me at a disadvantage. Humor was her choice weapon to ward off any necessary correction.

That little village seemed to be frozen in time with the church as the hub of community life. That little white building was the meeting place where life and death made their appointments with the people. Every year there was a church bazaar, a rummage sale, a box social, a Sunday school picnic, a sleigh ride for the teens and any number of excuses to bring people together. The older kids in the community devised creative ways to have fun. A group of teens occasionally tobogganed down the long winding hill onto the main street. Of course that was the road leading into the village, and such reckless behavior was forbidden by the mayor. He was a man of no nonsense whose face had been bruised by the bitter blows of time and therefore could be rather intimidating, especially to the youth.

One night, under a full moon, the teenagers set out for an evening of fun. Taking turns, one person always stood at the bottom of the hill to warn of coming traffic while the rest crowded onto the long toboggan and shoved off from the top of the mountain, accelerating as they tore around the curves at breakneck speed. This went on for a good while before someone reported the mischief to the mayor, who promptly pulled on his furs to deal with the situation. Just as he started up the hill in the dark, the toboggan was coming down and it was too late. The warning whistle was lost in the laughter and shrieks from the oncoming fury. As the toboggan rounded the last corner, it rammed into the poor man, scooping him into the lap of the girl at the front, while the rest of the crowd jumped off and rolled into the darkness of the landscape. At the bottom of the hill, she was left alone to explain her unconventional behavior to a visibly angry man.

Every winter, the church organized a sleigh ride for the teens in the area. That was a very popular tradition that drew large crowds. These social gatherings were always an opportunity to impress the opposite sex, especially since it took place in the evening. For that reason, the girls wore tight jeans and fancy boots and the guys would not be caught dead wearing a hat, in spite of the bitter cold. In those circumstances, it was impossible for us not to suspect some romantic attachments or what appeared to be sizeable strides in that direction. When the crowd from the boarding home was duly returned late in the evening, the rest of us who had missed the fun witnessed a most puzzling scene. Boots and gloves were removed amidst tears and sobs as the girls nursed frostbitten extremities. I wasn't sure that the guys had been terribly impressed by these girls' skimpy clothing, or recognized any tall order of wisdom in their wardrobe.

Judging from their swollen ears the next morning, I'm not certain that the boys had much to boast about either.

Another very popular event was the "box social" which was a fundraiser for the church. All the ladies who participated brought a creatively decorated box lunch to be auctioned off to the highest bidder. There seemed to be no limit to the ingenuity of these elaborate productions that could range from the boot of a nursery rhyme to an ornate basket with ribbons and bows. Great was the eagerness of all the young men to purchase the pretty box that belonged to the charming lady and share her lunch in the company of good friends. All in a friendly way, there was much merriment in the event, betting and teasing among the polished crowd. The young men tried to outbid each other for the privilege of sharing that lunch with the lady who, they hoped, had prepared it. Of course, there were always surprises. I was very proud when my teacher bought my box and we had lunch together. I remember one very pretty box that sold for over sixty dollars as two men vied for the coveted lady's presence, only to discover that the lunch belonged to an elderly widow. It was all in good fun and the church benefited from these generous bids.

The Sunday School picnic took place in June and was a day of fun for children of all ages. There were all manner of games and races, each highly entertaining, and rewards for Bible verses memorized. Everyone participated in the potato sack race, where each contestant was expected to hop the distance in a potato bag. The three-legged race was run with a partner, each having a leg tied to the other person and required cooperation and coordination. Ribbons and prizes were distributed and there was the great picnic lunch when everyone adjourned to a shady spot where the good things of the town were laid out to tempt the appetite. Mountains of sandwiches and cookies crowned the day for a crowd of squirmy kids.

There was a lake within walking distance of the boarding home, and earlier that winter, when it was beginning to freeze over, a half dozen of us kids had decided to check it out on a Saturday morning. We were sliding across the thin surface shouting with glee, when a lady spotted us and bribed us to her house with candy. When we had been appropriately scolded for such foolhardy behavior, we were sent back to our lodgings to face the music for our misdemeanor. We were reminded of the unspeakable grief we would have caused our parents had we fallen through the ice and drowned. By way of discipline, we were sent to bed for the entire day. Without a spoken word, but with much inward discomfort, we shuffled to our respective rooms. It must have been an effective punishment, because I have never forgotten the incident and still shudder when I think of what could have happened.

I remember that our little bedroom had a balcony with a fire escape. In winter, the bare branches of the towering maple, like bony fingers, scraped the railing by our window. The sound had a nightmarish quality that sent shivers up my spine. But of course, Mama was not around to appease my fears, so I learned to be brave at a very early age. Because I had been instructed to comfort my sister when she was sad or afraid, I refused to be intimidated by strange noises, for I had a responsibility here. From the day we were packed off to attend school, I developed a sense of independence and resourcefulness, which has remained with me over the years.

One morning I awoke with the intense desire to run along the ridge and through the woods to the waterfall behind our house; but when I opened my eyes, I realized that I was far from home and a deep sense of loneliness settled over me. It would be weeks before I would set eyes on those woods and run free again. The highlights of our lives were Mama's long letters that blanketed us in her warmth as she documented their lives back at the homestead.

It was February in 1950 when Yvonne was taken to the Montreal General Hospital. She had been suffering from gall bladder problems for years, but could not afford the treatment. At last she would receive the necessary surgery through the generosity of the Junior Red Cross, and she wrote to inform our matron of her scheduled hospitalization.

Thrust into the middle of any glorious day, an occasional tragedy can be injected. It so happened when one day Lizette and I were called downstairs to the minister's study. At the look of deep concern on our matron's face, disquieting thoughts crossed my mind. Could I be accused of an offence which, I was convinced, I lacked the resources to commit? Then my brother joined us and I realized that something serious was in the works. The good lady cleared her throat and tried to explain as gently as she could that she had received a phone call from Montreal requesting prayer for our mother who had just had surgery and had taken a turn for the worse. Dread landed flopping in my stomach as my mind raced to link the words with the reality they conveyed. "Your dear mother is so seriously ill that we are holding a special prayer meeting for her today. Many people will be praying for her recovery and I want you to do the same." At this point, she bowed her head and, with her arms around us, she kindly prayed for our precious Mama lying in a hospital bed so far away. Tears flowed freely as we realized what we stood to lose.

Several days passed before we learned of her recovery. The Lord had been gracious to spare her life and ease our pain. Letters from Papa kept us abreast of developments, as Mama spent six long weeks recovering in the hospital, to finally return home in time for Easter. We were more anxious than ever to see our dear Mama as we counted the days on the calendar to the Easter vacation. In hindsight, I am able to view that incident as a brief act in the grand manuscript of God's master plan for our lives, a time when He drew us close to comfort us.

As the days lengthened, children gathered in small groups to initiate new games. The attic contained a wealth of old garments. The dim light sent eerie shadows over miscellaneous shapes, plunging the gloomy corners into alarming darkness. Heaps of old boxes full of musty books, old clothes, boots and skates were strewn about. Before long, we were decked in the gaudy plumage of storybook royalty. Lords and ladies and peasants in strange costume, we played the role of nobility in all their pomp. On other days, we were cowboys and Indians or cops and robbers, depending on the mood and the weather. A combination of children and free time will inevitably produce imaginative schemes. As I recall, where imagination was a factor, we excelled. Thus engaged in work and play, we took little notice of time and days slipped by quickly.

In early spring, as winter loosened its icy grip, I loved to wander past the huddle of fir trees down to the river that marked the end of the property, just to watch the water rumbling its way around the bend and rushing to carry its overload downstream. That river had abandoned all pretence of flowing sedately and had gathered up its skirts as her angry waters came roaring down with a furious vengeance, carrying all manner of debris from upstream. The dark waters then disappeared behind a screen of sumac and willows to my left. Where and how far it carried its load, I never knew and often wondered, as I explored the rich underbrush, searching for treasures in the melting snow. Following heavy rains, spring bullied its way across the fields and the snow shrunk back, leaving delightful puddles in the schoolyard. Grass sprouted, timidly at first, but eventually painted the lawns green. A family of birds built their nest in the ledge over our balcony.

One must keep in mind that, at such a young age, I was only a quarter tame and a good portion of the backwoods remained anchored in my soul. Hence I often felt the need to escape to the balcony in the early morning to breathe deeply before being confined within the walls of our institution. One day I made an extraordinary find in the basket of clothespins - a mouse with wings! When I brought the soft furry thing into the dorm to show off my discovery, someone screamed, "Une chauve-souris!" (translated literally means 'bald mouse'). She had to be mistaken because that mouse had plenty of fur. Then I heard "Drop that thing!" and being obedient, I made my second mistake; I dropped the screeching bat, which took off around the room. As it fluttered about, the girls ran around, screaming and raising Cain. All the while, the poor creature was doing its best to keep off the dull times for them by fluttering within inches of their heads. Much to my consternation, I had mobilized an entire community, practically jumping out of their stockings. Brooms were flying, doors slamming, children screaming while I looked on, totally stunned. It was such a tiny creature. Much to my relief, it finally disappeared somewhere around the chimney and the world slowly returned to its normal pace. That day I learned a lesson that I was not about to forget, namely that "a bald mouse" is not welcome in a boarding home.

Some incidents would be best forgotten, but somehow have a way of remaining etched in our memories. The cleaning lady had left a bar of soap on the top step as she worked her way down the stairs with her pail. One of the employees came around the landing in a hurry and some of us witnessed a painful experience. The foot, which she placed on that bar of soap, flew eastward toward the rising sun and the other foot took off on a trip of its own toward the west. Her bottom landed on a step near the top of the stairs but did not remain there. It accelerated as it struck each step with a loud bump, creating visible concern all around. Somewhat embarrassed and very bruised, she tried to rearrange what very little was left of her dignity. She managed to carry on with her duties, avoiding chairs for several days. Had the victim complained, it would have been awkward for her to reveal the extent of her injuries.

Those long months away from home would leave yawning gaps in our lives. We grew taller, our feet got bigger, some teeth fell out and new ones grew in; all those ordinary marvelous things that Mama was missing. It was a life we were learning to accept in spite of its many drawbacks, not the least of which was homesickness.

Easter Vacation

A house is built of logs and stone,
Of tiles and posts and piers;
A home is built of loving deeds
That stand a thousand years. (Victor Hugo)

At last, winter reluctantly gave way to spring and another ten-day vacation at Easter provided a welcome break in the routine. Of course for us, it meant so much more than a few days off. We hoped that the spring thaw would not close the roads completely and bring disappointment. Almost four months had passed since our last visit home and our hearts ached to see our parents again.

Easter was late and the roads were muddy, but Papa managed to get the horse and wagon to the village, where he had parked the old car to drive the rest of the way. The drive northward to our village was just as jubilant as our Christmas trip except that the potholes bounced us a little higher. It felt as if all four wheels were never on the road at the same time. Papa was not a fast driver; it's just that the road was never a level playing field. It twisted and turned and slanted in many directions all at once so that the driver had to be alert and practiced to keep on track and out of the landscape. As passengers, we quickly learned to ride our precarious seat like a horse, holding on with both hands. As the road condition worsened, the old rattlebox burped over the bumps and sank into the deep ruts along the winding lane, groaning and sputtering. With the quick spring thaw, the deep quagmire, which Papa termed a "ventre de boeuf" (bull's belly), could quickly overcome all automotive power. We were fortunate that year to have made it safely to the village.

By the time we reached the parked horses, Leo had exhausted a full pack of cigarettes. We were duly transferred to the wagon where we settled down for the last several miles at a more relaxed pace. There was plenty of time to chat and catch up on the winter months from our respective agendas. About a half mile from the house, the water from the melting snow had risen some 60 centimetres above the road, so Papa and Yvon carried my sister and me on their shoulders to the foot of the hill. No sooner were we deposited than we scrambled up to the house where we knew Mama would be expecting her little brood. By the time we arrived, the day was growing old and the sun was lost in streamers of red and gold clouds fading in the western sky. How comforting to be held once again in her embrace, to share the stories and catch up on all we had missed since Christmas. The angry-looking scar across her abdomen bore testimony of her brush with death, and reminded us again of God's goodness to our family.

The days were milder now and the melting snow fed the cascade in the woods behind the house, that tiny stream skipping over rocks as it threaded its way down to the valley below, the one that I had dreamed about during my long absence. I breathed deeply of the delicious fragrance of the day. Large chunks of lingering snow were pocketed in the folds of the huge boulders to the west, feeding little rivulets and streams loosed from their shackles of ice. There was a feeling of warmth and freedom in the clear, crisp air like a touch of the resurrection in the depths of the soul. It was exhilarating to run free and revisit those familiar landmarks and drink from that icy waterfall, as the water gurgled merrily over the rocks through deep mossy woods. It was a peaceful, quiet spot where wild flowers embroidered the green canvas of the ridge with their fragile beauty every year. When I called out to my sister, the wind seemed to catch the words and send them flying over the field. In the absence of traffic, I felt that the quietness was almost sacred in these parts. The air was filled with the smell of spring, and the sun felt so warm that we removed our shoes and ran barefoot until Mama cornered us and made sure we were properly bundled against the cool wind, reminding us that as long as there is snow on the ground, we must keep our feet covered.

The night was warm with spring when a spiteful little wind

sprang up splattering the window panes. The dance of the rain on the tin roof played in harmony with the chirping frogs that were just awakening from their long winter sleep. Mama called it God's music. By morning the wind had increased to gale force, screaming around the windows and shaking the house frightfully. A cold rain ticked as it pelted against the windows, journeying from a distant gray sky. I noticed that Papa was smoking more feverishly when, suddenly the house lifted from its moorings and landed with a loud thud. It was downright scary! The following summer, he anchored the house to the ground with a steel cable.

Content to be clothed in Mama's embrace, the days sped by in a maze of down-home warmth, maple syrup, hot bread, purring kettle, and warm cuddles. We could already feel the first gentle touch of summer's fingers. The days were longer and the indigo-blue evening sky was loaded with stars. The peace and serenity of our vacation would soon be punctured by the sharp edge of reality and our return to school. Leaving was less traumatic this time in the knowledge that the summer vacation was only two months away, when we would be back for a long holiday. Just as the first flocks of wild geese flew northward, and the daffodils prepared to toss their yellow heads in the breeze, we were heading back to school for our final semester.

Until departure, the hours loomed blankly. The sky was overcast and before long, the road was half hidden behind a curtain of rain, the bleak surroundings doing little to lighten our spirits. Where the road was paved, it gleamed like patent leather in the falling rain. Where it was not paved, mud was a factor. The drive stretched into hours as we wound our way through the haze that blanketed the atmosphere. With every departure, I gathered in my mind the kaleidoscope of colour that had brought joy to our lives during those brief vacations. Happiness would linger as a distant memory when loneliness set in. Those early experiences left me with a better understanding of lonely people. They are not just statistics but real people with faces, families, emotions, hopes and dreams. I can empathize because I've been there myself. That spring semester would end for us the first of many years away from home.

Piano Lessons

Reach high, for stars lie hidden in your soul.
Dream deep, for every dream precedes the goal.
(P.V.Starr)

Someone got the bright idea that I should take piano lessons with the local pianist. I understood that I was given a rare privilege reserved for a few very special people, so it was with pride that I headed out for my very first lesson. I walked the length of the village, past the general store, the post office, the gas station and then beyond the butter factory, I climbed the long winding hill to an impressive Victorian house. The white building stood dignified and stately on its vantage point overlooking the village. To a child, it looked like a palace of rich nobles with lush grounds stretching down over the hillside. It belonged to a founding family in the community. The old gentleman operated a water-powered sawmill providing employment for a number of men in the small locality. These folks were descendants of Huguenots from Belgium and fiercely guarded their French Protestant roots. They were very involved in the local church.

At the gate that pierced the royal enclosure, my eyes grew big with wonder and delight, as my heart beat faster. I remember walking in the shade of an impressive stone fence along a path that led to a screen door on the other side of the house. I stood for a moment, waiting for my pounding heart to behave. When I knocked timidly, I heard shuffling footsteps approaching. The door opened and I was ushered into an antique kitchen, where I was greeted with warm smiles and the aroma of fresh cookies. The ancient clock on the opposite wall displayed Roman numerals and clearly pointed to 3:30. Was I an hour early? The kind lady explained that her husband refused to move to daylight saving time, considering it nonsense. The old man spent his days outdoors and worked with the sun, hence standard time.

These old folks were a charming couple in their late seventies. The kind lady's warm smile accented her wrinkles into crevices through which, it seemed to me, her very soul might slip. She took my hand and led me to the table where a plate of warm cookies and a glass of milk were laid out. I felt as if I had just climbed to paradise. She inquired about my family and the small talk gradually dissipated my apprehensions.

As I munched on those delightful treats, I tried to take in the details of that magnificent dwelling. A classmate of mine had been asked to deliver a package to this house. When she returned with the same package in hand, she explained that she had not found the house, for there was only a castle at the top of the hill. Now I understood her conclusion, for this had to be more than a house. Perhaps it was a mansion after all.

Their daughter, Aline, who was on the downhill side of her forties at the time, was slim and elegant and wore a soft perfume. The upholstered cheerfulness of the dining room calmed my apprehensions as she led me into the living room, on the north side of the house where the heavily draped windows looked out on a long veranda that held its own twilight. The furniture was dark wood and the walls a weary shade of green. With its burden of furnishings, the room seemed to soak up the light and turn it dull. We sat at the piano where my teacher patiently explained the rudiments of music. When her fingers poured over the keys, my soul stood in silence. Her music was sheer magic. The base notes grumbled like soft thunder in the distance and the high notes played a joyful dance. With little effort, she could set the piano in an uproar. I wondered whether I would ever solve this great mystery and master the instrument. It certainly promised to be an exciting challenge. The lesson was soon over and I had my first assignment.

As I walked through the dining room and back to the kitchen, the sun seemed to pour into the windows like butter. I contented myself with polite noises and left. On my way back, I doubt that my feet touched the gravel. With my music book tucked safely under my arm, I was flying. That night when I knelt by my bed, I prayed for my piano teacher that God would let nothing happen to her except "what's nice". Looking back to those happy times, I remember her and her family as real gems from my memory book.

Summer

Lord, if I'm feeling rushed today,
I need your eyes to help me see
That when an interruption comes,
It is an opportunity. (Sper)

By mid June, we were packing again and, as we left, I recall how our bedroom wore a bleak, purged look, shorn of all but essentials. We said our farewells to teachers and friends with little emotion, for we would be back. We were homeward bound for two whole months of sheer joy, when everything seemed blessed with the fullness of life and the will to live.

Back in those early days, when we were still only a quarter tamed, we removed all footwear in spring and ran barefoot until the frosts of September. It was not many days before the sole of our feet turned to leather, and we could run over sharp rocks and freshly mown hay without any discomfort. The only time I really needed any shoes was to pick wild raspberries, which always abounded in thick brambles or heavy brush. To this day I recall my frantic efforts to extract myself from the clutches of giant raspberry bushes. Every year when raspberry season called for us to pick in the underbrush, Mama expressed her fear of wild animals. She suspected that a bear might decide that a child looked more like a snack than a threat, and she warned us appropriately, though I am not certain that any of us knew how to deal with that possibility.

Summers were a busy time on the homestead. Papa spent all of July harvesting hay and oats to winter the horses, while Mama tended an immense garden that provided most of our fresh food. We children were also expected to pick berries of every variety to make jam. Money was scarce, but none of us even suspected that anything less than the abundance of the Almighty was ours. As Papa once said, we were rich; it's only money we didn't have. Usually in the midst of this busy season, our relatives from the city dropped in without warning.

One fine day, when the fields shimmered in the heat of the July sun, a day when the call of summer can be more seductive than the call to work, we were all busy weeding the garden. Mama had promised to take us to the lake for a swim if we each weeded one row of vegetables. I was in charge of the onions, which was quite straightforward. Mama took on the tiny carrots or beets, which were hard to distinguish among the weeds. Yvon hoed the potatoes and beans, while Lizette weeded around the tomato plants. As we worked, the heat wrapped itself around us like a blanket, and even the cheerfulness of the crickets was oppressive. We made frequent trips to the dipper resting in a water bucket on a crippled chair by the garden gate. Our surface well supplied us with beautiful, cold, clear water, which was never so deeply appreciated as on such days. My thoughts carried me back to the previous summer when my uncle had brought his family from Montreal to spend two weeks with their country cousins. At first we had been excited to see them, but after a few days, I needed my space and I had staked out a claim in the abandoned chicken coop. That had become my secret hideout when I felt the need to get away.

I recalled the day my cousin decided to ride the old workhorse bareback in the pasture. Old Fred was born with a down-hearted look and seemed to perk up only when we were around. A horse can be controlled from the front end, but from the rear, you never know what kind of an impression they can make. Dom pretended to be the Lone Ranger and complained that old Fred was too slow, so Yvon had taken out his BB gun and given him a ride to remember. When he picked himself up, our young cowboy mumbled, "I had never realized that the back of a horse was so far from the ground!" After a wild gallop, old Fred had cast a resentful glance over his shoulder, and resumed his grazing further down the field. He was the same lad who had sat down on Mama's bread dough that just happened to be rising in a large covered dish on a kitchen chair. As I recall, Mama did not share his amusement at the time. I wondered whether they would return this year. Visitors always generated some excitement for us as we took them fishing and swimming whenever we could get away. It was our way of showing off our skills to the city folks. We also had to make considerable adjustments to find sleeping accommodations for everyone. Visitors inevitably caused quite a stir, for even the chickens announced their important presence to newcomers.

Just then we heard the roar of an engine climbing the steep hill. Mama dusted off her knees and hurried towards the house. Her face was red with perspiration, and she ordered us to wash up and change our grubby clothes. At these words, we were galvanized into action, and we had hardly cleared the front steps, when a red car appeared over the ridge. Panic! In such cramped quarters, it was easy to get into one another's way, and you sometimes met yourself coming through the door. Mama quickly pulled on a pair of clean socks in an effort to conceal the offending extremities. She would wash up later.

Mama was the first to greet our guests while we kids rushed about in the safety of the house. We each grabbed a facecloth and scrubbed the exposed skin, before slipping on something clean. Upon close inspection, we might have appeared somewhat scruffy, but in the excitement, such details were surely overlooked. Our prettiest outfits were worn on our countenance, just a radiant smile. Not only had these unexpected guests put an end to our gardening chores, they would bring a refreshing change into our lives.

Night of Terror

If God seems far away, guess who moved.

A whole carload of relatives had arrived from the city, all women. In those days they had to be a brave lot to drive the 125 miles north into the boonies, the last 25 miles being a challenge to any motorist. Those were the days when Maurice Duplessis was premier of Quebec and any constituency that did not vote for the party in power, namely the Union Nationale, was denied road repairs. Consequently, road conditions were a clear reflection of the county's political tendencies, and ours was no exception. By all evidence we favored the opposition.

We were thrilled to have visitors because we knew that they were prepared to spend at least a week in the country by way of vacations, a term used only by city folk and totally unknown to farmers. It would, however, allow us to slow our pace to entertain our guests, something we inevitably enjoyed. That is as close as we ever got to experiencing a vacation back then.

There was Aunt Rose who drove the heavy Buick. She donned a bright red dress, no doubt the latest fashion from Morgan's downtown. Antoinette was so ritzy that she would never blend into the context of our farm. With some effort, Annette might fit in, as she was less fussy than her sisters. How Jacqueline was ever persuaded to come was beyond my imagination; she was afraid of her own shadow and would need a good dose of survival skills to live out the week. Flore was a clown and kept everyone rolling with laughter. They all looked very attractive indeed in their pretty clothes, new hairstyles and bright nail polish and lipstick for these were our city counterparts, the fashionable ones, and we were appropriately impressed.

Following the initial greetings and comments on how much we had grown, we scrambled to prepare a decent meal.

A small house required efficiency where the main floor served as kitchen, living room and dining room. Without a refrigerator, the garden provided most of the fresh produce and the meat came from the chicken house. While Lizette proudly showed off the garden to our guests, Mama made her way to the chicken coop. She unceremoniously grabbed a large fowl by the feet, and carried the squawking creature with wings flapping to the butchering block. There in a cloud of feathers, she proceeded to transform the protesting bird into a plump chicken for dinner. Of course our visitors were too sensitive to witness such a crime so it was my lot to help pluck the feathers and clean up the mess. It took only a few minutes and the deed was done.

Before long the aroma of roast chicken and freshly baked bread emanated from the oven of the wood stove. The ladies helped to prepare the vegetables amidst peels of laughter as they shared the adventures of their trip; like taking a wrong turn and driving along a deserted stretch of road to a logging camp. As the pitch rose, I concluded that it was not unlike the sound of the chicken coop.

It was hot in the little kitchen when everyone sat around the table for dinner as there was no ceiling fan to stir the air, but somehow that could not spoil the feast. The chatter continued until Papa lit the kerosene lamps and the dishes were washed with hot water from the kettle. Night had fallen and the young moon hung low in the west when Papa showed our guests to the little cottage on the ridge reserved for company. The evening breeze was soft and warm, whispering its way across the wooded hillside as they walked together. Only the occasional giggle in the distance broke the silence when we turned in for the night. It had been an eventful day on the farm and, totally exhausted, we all fell into a deep sleep.

Meanwhile in the cottage, the ladies settled in too, but their isolation made them uneasy. The flickering lamp cast eerie shadows on the walls and their own reflections in the windows made them jump. Antoinette and Rose had grown up on a farm, but that had been many years ago and not in the back woods like this place. Now both sisters were fashionable hairdressers in downtown Montreal, a far cry from this. To make matters worse, the light attracted sandflies, those invisible pests that can pass through screens and torment you like mosquitoes. This called for lights out, and the fears of the visible were replaced by the fears of the invisible. The nocturnal sounds of the forest, the chirping frogs and crickets, and the call of the whippoorwill all blended together into a symphony peculiar to summer nights in the country. Perhaps the absence of screaming traffic and city lights sharpened their awareness of the night, for the girls could not sleep. The occasional howl in the distance sounded threatening. What if something climbed in through the window!

Then it happened. There was a loud cracking sound and the cottage shifted. Everyone was wide-eyed and tense. "What was that?" "Shh...Listen!" They were whispering as they drew the blankets up. Another tremor was followed by a snort; and then, more scratching and loud grunting just beneath the bedroom window. There could be no doubt about it; this had to be a bear trying to break in. They had heard about such tragedies in remote areas. Without a word, the girls in the bed nearest the window joined the others, and all five huddled together in the same bed, shaking with fright. They were too far from the house to call for help, and of course, there was no telephone. Such primitive conditions! The heavy breathing subsided, and then seemed to move away; but in the cottage, no one dared to move. The threat was still very real.

Subdued whispers continued late into the night as the moonlight slipped silently over the bed and shifted to the little kitchen. It was hot under the blanket, but moving was out of the question in the dead of night. So the minutes ticked by and the chirping of the frogs died down. Even the whippoorwill flew off and there was an uncanny silence in the forest. "Perhaps the danger has passed and we can sleep." suggested Annette, who was squeezed in the middle of the bed. No one moved. It might come back!

"It must be your perfume, Jacqueline."

"You talk too much. It was all your squealing that attracted that animal!"

"No way! Bears have poor hearing."

"Listen, it's back! The cottage began to shake again and this time the snorting was distinctly louder as an ominous shadow darkened the little window.

"Mon Dieu! It's coming for us!" whimpered Rose. Another cracking sound from the foundation of the building and the whole cottage shook. This thing meant business.

"What can we do if it breaks in?" cried Jacqueline, for whom this was a second visit to the North.

"Just pray that it doesn't come for us."

"Did you lock the door when you came in?"

"It has only a padlock on the outside and doesn't lock from the inside. Let's hope the bear doesn't know that." There was a nervous giggle, but no one really thought it was funny. In spite of the heat under the blanket, the ladies were shivering. Once again the sound of heavy steps retreating towards the woods brought a sigh of relief from the crowded bed; yet no one moved.

Then quite abruptly, the silence was broken by a new melody. The birds were singing their morning songs. As the darkness faded into gray, fear lost its grip and the dreaded beast of the night was less threatening now. The whistling of a rollicking tune from the house reminded the girls that they were not alone. Annette was the first to get up and peek out of the window. A thick mist covered the fields, but she could hear Papa bringing in the cow for milking. The scene was peaceful with the old horse grazing nearby. Could that nightmare have been a figment of their imagination?

"Where is the bathroom around here?"

"There is only an outhouse at the back near the woods."

"There's no way I'm going out there alone! We need help." It was at that point that we heard Annette calling Papa. He left the cow and walked up the hill, wondering what was wrong. He had never had such a warm reception by so many females before. He told us later that he felt like a rooster in a henhouse. By the time each one had had her say, it was hard to tell who was relating the incident and who was interrupting. It took a while for the commotion to sort itself out, but when he was able to decipher their dilemma, he went on a tour of inspection.

Night of Terror

"Let me check around for tracks. Aha...It was a big one all right...probably 1600 pounds, I'd guess. It left some hair on the wall where you heard all the noise." At these words, our guests paled and looked at each other knowingly.

"It's no wonder the whole building shook. A beast that size would have no trouble breaking through the wall." hissed Rose.

"It just needed a good scratch. The mosquitoes are pesky here at night. But it wouldn't break in."

"How can you be so sure? It sounded frightful and snorted threateningly." chimed in the others.

"That's normal; they always do that when they scratch." added Papa calmly.

"Well, I'm not spending another night here, not with 1600-pound bears trying to break in; no way! I'm going home."

"Bears? Follow me, Ladies. Bears aren't all bad. There's the cause of all your grief. This is Fred."

"The workhorse? Do you mean to say that it was this animal that kept us awake all night?" Each looked accusingly at the other as they realized how foolish they had been. When we heard the detailed account of their night of terror, it dawned on me that they had had all the initiation they needed for the summer and we should not add to their sorrows with our usual pranks. That morning I learned an important lesson too. I decided that I would never live in fear of the unknown, and to this day, when I hear strange noises in the night, I get up and check it out. I've discovered that my bears usually turn into horses too.

Haying

Who reaps the grain and plows the sod,
Must feel a kinship with his God...
The man who breathes fresh country air
Must know full well that God is there.
(R.W. Stuart)

Recently we were stacking hay in our own barn when my son complained that haying had to be the hardest job in such oppressive heat. I assured him that things had improved since I was his age. The heat was the same back then, only the tools were considerably more primitive and conditions more harrowing.

Our farm presented an uneven playing field, a rocky hillside indented by tangled hollows, and dotted with stumps. Farm machinery was useless, so the only solution was to mow the hay by hand with a long-handled scythe. As soon as the dew was gone, Papa left for the fields where he worked under the scorching sun, cutting wide swaths of hay in a semi-circular movement, inching his way across the rough landscape he called the "Land of Cain". He stopped at intervals to sharpen the long blade of the scythe with strong rasping strokes. His only pieces of equipment were his scythe, an emery stone in his pocket and a gallon of drinking water, which he drained and as quickly sweated through his pores. He had to keep a sharp lookout for rocks and wasps' nests, both hazards to be avoided. When he spotted a wasp nest on the ground, he left a tuft of hay standing to mark the spot and avoid further contact.

Of course this work depended on favorable weather. Once cut, the hay was left to dry in the sun, then turned over with a pitchfork to dry another day before raking and stacking it in mounds on the field. On the third day, these mounds had to be loaded on the wagon. How well I remember Mama on top of the load driving the team of horses at a perilous angle on the mountainside. Papa disappeared beneath huge mounds of hay as he pitched each pile onto the wagon. The higher the load, the more effort was required, and the more short-tempered he became under the blistering sun. When things went wrong, Mama was usually the target of his cussing. His clothes were dripping with perspiration, but the threat of rain usually accelerated the pace.

As there were no baby-sitters, we children were always part of the action. Our job was to rake up the hay left under those piles as they were removed. I even have a snapshot of me at two months old in a basket in the shade of a tree in the hayfield. One day when Lizette was only three, she stumbled across a wasp nest in the field. The poor child was stung in 17 places on her little body. Miraculously she did not go into shock, but I remember my parents' deep concern for her at the time. It remained a hard-earned lesson for all of us. Haying was an all-consuming project for pioneer families that lasted a good part of the summer.

Sudden summer storms have always been a real threat to harvesting good hay, and, I remember, at a very young age, racing to the barn and opening wide the doors to let the horses in with a wagon load just in time to avoid a downpour. It was always a struggle to shut those massive doors against the powerful gusts of wind that threatened to rip them off their hinges. Until Papa installed a special contraption to unload the hay, it had to be unloaded with the same pitchfork and stored in the barn to feed the horses and cows in the winter. No matter how I look at it, life in the 1940s was an ongoing battle against the elements, and pioneers had to be made of tough material.

The story bore little difference when harvesting the oats in late summer. That was before the invention of the combine (at least in our area) when the grain had to be mowed like the hay, tied in sheaves and stacked until the arrival of the threshing crew. These were solid wind-worn men in the full vigour of their mid thirties who traveled from farm to farm with an old threshing machine that hooked up to a stationary engine with a wide belt. Papa used an ancient Hudson motor to operate such machinery. The big engine groaned

Haying

and coughed and suddenly roared to life. It was in an ear-piercing roar and a cloud of dust that the grain was bagged and then stored in the barn. The straw was pitched into the loft for animal bedding. Finally the engine slowed to a stop, heaving a great hiss from its iron innards. It was time for vittles, when everyone came into the house to wash up and savor one of Mama's feasts. That was usually accompanied by a friendly glass of homemade wine and capped with a hot blueberry cobbler bathed in fresh cream. Homemade brew always solved the problem of the absence of a convenient and affordable liquor store where one might find a good bottle of wine.

The laughter increased in pitch and volume as the wine glasses were refilled and the men shared a succession of stories, each one funnier than the one before. One of these fellows stood out. His teeth looked very white in the jungle of his hairy face, and his laughter was contagious. I'll never forget the story about two men who lived some five miles up the road from our place. It seems that each of these gentlemen got along better with the wife of the other. One day they decided to swap wives. By today's standards, this may not sound very strange, but because one of the women had a limp, the man who accepted her demanded some compensation from the former husband. It sounded to me like they had exchanged horses. Some of the tales we heard on such occasions were so funny that the men nearly laughed their bones loose. It was a most effective way of relieving stress and, in spite of the hard work, no one complained. I recall, as darkness fell and the men pulled away from the table, they left with a smile.

The Storm

The lightning of a summer storm
Its thunder roaring in reply,
Reveal to us an awesome God
Whose power we can't deny. (Sper)

One Sunday Papa took the family fishing on Lac des Iles, a large lake dotted with numerous islands. Mama packed a picnic lunch and we headed out for a rare adventure. On the way we hit a squirrel. That animal had to be blind or suicidal because Papa rarely exceeded 30 mph on those roads. To reach our destination, we had to cross Lac Napoleon and portage about a half mile through the woods. We left the truck by the lake and loaded our primitive equipment, including a bucket of minnows and some worms into a rowboat among half a dozen similar vessels that slumbered at their moorings like sleeping elders. It promised to be one of those golden days to store up as treasure for the future.

The soft splashing of the oars created a little rhythm and the slow pace allowed us to catch a glimpse of the loons that were busy nesting by the shore. We passed an occasional summer property where folks waved a greeting. Of a lavish place, Papa explained that some wealth had trickled down to its owners, who enjoyed a more affluent lifestyle than most of their contemporaries in these parts. The sun was just pulling itself up to a sitting position, spilling warmth upon the waking world, when it poured a golden dial of light across the water that seemed to point to our destination.

The August morning was an hour older when we reached the shore at the far end of the lake. In a screen of foliage at the north end, the deep waters were dark and still and a little frightening. Papa tied the boat to a tree and distributed its contents to everyone. Then he led the way and we stumbled along behind him Indian file following an invisible trail, which Papa instinctively discerned. It was quite dim under the tall trees and the underbrush was still wet with dew. Of course we knew enough to keep a safe distance between us to avoid getting a branch in the face. Just as our packs were feeling too heavy to go on, we spotted a light at the end of the tunnel. We had reached the second lake where another rowboat was moored.

We proceeded to empty the vessel of its load of collected rainwater. Then we cleaned off the seats and loaded our baggage for the adventure ahead. In case that little rowboat intended to leak, we brought along the buckets to circumvent her suicidal tendencies. Because he was familiar with the lake, Papa paddled toward a big island offshore, where we scrambled up on the rocks and tried out our fishing gear. We did get some nibbles and caught a few perch and sunfish, but exploring the shoreline proved to be as much fun as trying to catch fish. Of course, the thick undergrowth kept us close to the water where we were intrigued by the many shells and tiny creatures moving among the rocks. The air was alive with birds and crickets, but the lake, unruffled by wind, had turned from blue to the translucence of mother of pearl in the midday sun. By lunchtime we were ravenous, and eating on a rock surrounded by water was like a storybook adventure. This day was turning out to be the best.

Papa's voice called us back to the boat, where we loaded our gear and headed to another fishing spot farther out. That, he promised, was a fisherman's paradise. We headed east around the island and continued on for a considerable distance. Somewhere, known only to Papa, we dropped anchor and resumed our fishing, with minnows for bait. This time it was serious business. We were pulling in big game, fighting bass and walleye that flopped around in the bottom of the rowboat. So excited was Papa with his catch that he forgot to light the cigarette that hung from his lips. I noticed then that the birds had ceased their chattering and were flying just a whisper above the trees. The sun was dipping behind the island and it was urgent that we leave the shelter of the bay and head back to shore before dark. A well-defined, ominous black mass with huge silver-gray puffy tops was growing on the western horizon.

As we rounded the island, the wind picked up and the earlier calm surface of the water was whipped up into white-caps. Rowing faster now against the breeze, Papa commented on the unusually warm air. As we approached the shore, I noticed the birds hurling themselves into the arms of the wind from the tossing branches of the trees. We quickly grabbed our bags including the heavy fish and headed into the woods, much darker now and more frightening. The night was falling fast and our only flashlight was losing heart, but Papa instinctively knew the way and we followed, running to keep up. We had another lake to cross before driving home and the wind was now push and shove.

When we reached the shore at the end of the portage, the clouds seemed to rise as a bear on hind legs and growl. The rowboat we had left there in the morning was already tugging willfully at her tether. We tumbled in and pushed away from shore. Papa grabbed the oars and pulled with all his might. From my vantage point as a six-year-old, the lake was transformed into a mutinous sea, as the wind churned the once glassy surface of the lake into a mountain range of snow-capped waves, rising and falling in tune with the kettledrums of thunder. We hugged the shoreline heading west, but the squall was slowing our progress. The restless water kept heaving our little vessel dangerously close to the rocks, as we bounced in a perilous drunken dance. With each gust of wind and every clap of thunder, I shuddered. I didn't even pretend to be brave; I was white-knuckle scared. From inky blackness to blinding flashes of lightning, we were only halfway across the lake when the rain was swept down in sheets. Thunderstorms had always frightened me even from the safety of the house, but this was the first time that I was smack in the middle of such madness. With no place to take shelter, we plowed straight ahead with the rain lashing and whipping at our faces.

When at last a flash of lightning revealed that our destination was just ahead, the wind hushed, a canyon opened in the clouds and stars appeared. The storm had passed. Such freak summer squalls are not uncommon in these parts, and they can wreak havoc and cause serious damage. When at last we abandoned ship and made for the car, we realized that we had been fortunate to escape injury. Dripping wet, we arrived home with our catch and a memorable experience to share with friends in the days ahead. Of course, our adventure did nothing to lessen my fear of thunderstorms, and to this day I pay close attention to the weather forecast when planning serious outdoor activities.

The House by the Lake

Some people think they have it all
When riches come their way;
But their great loss will be revealed
On God's accounting day. (Bosch)

During our summer vacation, my sister and I often delivered fresh eggs or a chicken that Mama had "undressed" for someone's dinner. This was one of Yvonne's sidelines to make extra cash. Most customers were delighted to have fresh produce, but I recall one customer who complained about the large bones in the chicken, preferring only meat. Mama's reply, "I've been trying to grow them boneless for years, but they keep falling over." These deliveries allowed us to visit friends and sometimes meet new folks who owned summer residences along the lakes nearby.

On one such errand, when I was perhaps eight or nine years old, we had to locate an attractive cottage nestled among the trees overlooking the water, some three kilometers away. We thought that the road must have followed an ancient moose trail and by its winding curves, my sister deduced that the moose was either blind or drunk. I knocked timidly at first, but when there was no response, we walked around to the veranda facing the lake. We were greeted warmly by a tall gentleman who wore his baldness like an expensive hat. His eyes had a disturbing luminescence, like gray clouds lit by a wintry sun, that couldn't focus. He spoke with stiff precision as if he were creeping through a verbal minefield. His talkative wife ushered us in to rest awhile from our long walk. Theirs was a fairly new house with a bright sunny kitchen that opened onto the screened porch overlooking the water. She insisted on showing us the rest of their pretty cottage, which I thoroughly enjoyed. As we observed the extravagance all around, I was reminded of Papa's words: "People buy things they don't need with money they don't have to impress neighbors they don't like."

The living room walls wore flowered wallpaper, the sort that one could refer to as a bee's nightmare. Across from the fireplace a variety of animal mounts stared down at us, giving me goose bumps. While we sat marveling at the view, the kind lady offered us a cool drink of something sweet, and in her high-pitched voice she assaulted my ears with a torrent of words, which I could only describe as a verbal tornado. She could talk 90 words a minute with gusts up to 180. I understood that they were recovering from a series of tragedies and had taken refuge in this quiet valley. She proceeded to explain, in what she fondly imagined was a whisper, that her husband had turned silently to the bottle to gain consolation from past tribulations and strength to face those to come. I had noticed that he had some booze aboard himself when we arrived. Now I understood why as their story unraveled in that quiet retreat and we were introduced to the faces that looked out from the framed photographs over the mantle. I concluded that these were genuine people with real heartaches, and not just tourists with extra cash. They had escaped from the city where life had been an endless journey burdened with sorrows, and in so doing, had spent a good deal of money trying to push all sadness from their lives; yet the emptiness remained.

With our glasses empty, we guessed it was time to leave, so I made the correct noises of appreciation and we left our hostess. We headed for the porch, where the tall gentleman rose and gave me a knuckle-grinding handshake by way of appreciation, and opened the screen door for our exit. Somewhat relieved, we escaped and quickly walked back to the main road. Silence was our companion as we ambled along, and I realized that on our homestead, we had only innocent sorrows to wear us down. We had each other and that was "riches" enough for me.

Stocking Up

There are two goals in life,
First to get what you want,
And after that, to enjoy it.
Only the wisest of mankind achieve the second.
(L.P. Smith)

Winter never completely lost its grip on our remote community, but it paused from mid-June to late August, when our garden was safe from frost. This was also the period for gathering and stocking up for winter. Where Papa had cleared ten acres from a neighboring woodlot, the wild strawberries abounded. They generally ripened in late June and early July, which coincided with the beginning of haying. As soon as the hay was cut, we launched into berry picking. One Sunday was usually dedicated to serious picking, when we brought a picnic lunch and spent the day in the field. To protect her from the relentless blessing of the sun, Mama wore a big straw hat, which Papa referred to as a cow's breakfast. We were all covered in an assortment of protective gear against the sun and the black flies. Like locusts we covered that field, filling our containers, and by evening, we had managed to fill three large buckets. Considering the size of the berries and the four-gallon pails, I still marvel at our achievement.

When at last we headed home, there remained one major hurdle to cross; that mountain of sweet berries had to be hulled. After the supper dishes had been cleared away, the painstaking task began, and continued late into the night by the dim light of the oil lamp. When we were too tired to be of any help, Mama sent us off to bed and continued the task with Papa. Their voices mingled with the symphony of the nocturnal creatures outside our window, as we fell into a sound sleep. The following day, the sweet aroma of strawberry jam filled the house, as dozens of jars were filled and sealed for the winter months. If the angels in heaven did not know what strawberry jam was, they certainly must have been curious by the time Mama got through and that sweet aroma wafted skyward.

The same ritual was repeated with raspberries, and in late summer with blueberries. In spite of the long hours of picking, we were very grateful for God's bountiful provision of wild berries. Yvonne untiringly preserved this abundance every year for our family to be used on pancakes and homemade bread as well as a variety of desserts with whipped cream. The jars found their way to the cellar where the potatoes, carrots, and turnips would all be gathered in the fall. That is how we raced the approaching winter months, and as I recall, no one has ever made such delightful jam since those sweet delicacies of my childhood. When she ran out of jars, Mama brewed the rest of the harvest, be it chokecherries, beets, and anything else that might otherwise spoil, into wine. Those bottles found their way to the cellar to emerge on special occasions. For that reason, the absence of supermarkets was a matter of no concern to us.

As autumn's shawl was slowly slipping over summer's hours, it was time to order new shoes and school supplies from Eaton's catalogue for the next school year. We were leaving with a mixture of delight and misery, anticipating a new beginning, yet reluctant to give up the freedom of summer and leave behind those we loved. With winter whispering in their wings, the swallows were leaving their nests and congregating along the radio antenna wire linking the house to the barn, in preparation for their yearly migration, much as we were doing. This would be an annual ritual in our home for many years, as time added chapters to our lives. With every departure I gathered in my mind the kaleidoscope of color that had brought us joy during those brief vacations. Happiness lingered as a distant memory when homesickness would set in. Those early sorrows left me with a better understanding of lonely people who, after all, are not just statistics or lists of names in an institution, but real people with

Stocking Up

---

faces, families, emotions, hopes and dreams. I understand, because I've been there.

> Now in the haze of leaf-smoke
> As summer fades from view,
> I lift my eyes
> to somber skies
> And die a little too. (Anon)

A Hair-Raising Experience

Your thunder was heard in the whirlwind,
Your lightening lit up the world;
The earth trembled and shook. (Psalms 77: 18)

One summer when Papa was away working in the Arctic region, Yvon decided to try his hand at logging and clearing land to earn money. He involved his sisters to carry branches and pile them up into huge mounds that resembled beaver huts. I don't recall much money resulting from all that labor, but I do remember one traumatizing experience. It was the day he had gone out to the forest wearing Papa's good Hamilton wristwatch, which had been a gift from the company he had worked for. Realizing his mistake, he carefully removed it and placed it on a stump, intending to retrieve it at the end of the day.

When Yvon lumbered home for supper, he realized that he had left the watch behind. The evening was sagging into the clutches of an approaching storm. He looked beat and turned to me, begging me to fetch the wretched thing before it rained. The sky darkened and the leaves began to shiver. A storm was definitely growing in the west. With the wind rising, a sense of urgency was heavy upon me to save the confounded watch. Why own something of value if it served only to cause so much trouble? After some hesitation, I decided to make a run for it. Close to a mile separated me from my goal, so I tore across the field and down the hill towards the road that led to the clearing in question. I noticed swarms of barn swallows flushed into the sky as I pursued my race toward the woods.

As I entered the darkened forest, the light filtered green and dense as the spreading limbs arched together to form a vaulted ceiling over a floor of leaves strewn with branches and twigs. How the wind did scream and the trees thrash around! Then a flash of lightning was followed by a whack-boom-rumble-boom-boom as the monster grumbled away into the darkening woods. I shuddered as the forest around me bowed under the force of the growing squall. When I finally sorted out which stump held the coveted watch, I grabbed it, and gripping it securely in my hand, I tried to outrun the approaching fury, but before I had reached the road, the downpour caught me full force. With no place to hide, I felt the icy grip of terror swelling in the pit of my stomach, crowding the very breath out of my lungs. The pressure seemed to cut off the beating of my heart. I had never been brave, and I was not about to prove otherwise that day. In my thinking, it is better to be chicken than a dead duck, though a duck of any kind might have fared better than I in that rain. Finally, exhausted and breathless, I collapsed in the safety of the porch clutching the cause of all my trouble. I did not share my brother's amusement at my appearance, but I held no grudge, as together we sat in the safety of the porch, and the storm swept over us, flashing and booming its way over our heads. Within an hour the rain had swallowed itself back up into the clouds and the sun emerged briefly to wrap up the day and fold it into the western escarpment.

By morning the birds sang joyfully to welcome us back to the woods that had been washed clean and wore their glorious summer dress. Life would go on, with my adventure of the previous night only a bad memory, adding another paragraph to my childhood.

Solitude

Not only is a woman's work never done,
the definition keeps changing.

In the early fifties, cordwood was being replaced by fuel oil for heating large buildings, and consequently, the price of firewood dropped. Leo found temporary jobs in Montreal and kept busy working for tourists in the summer months. In 1953 he signed a contract with a company to work in Northern Canada. He would be away for seven months in Goose Bay, Labrador earning big wages. This temporary solution held a promise of better days ahead, but it meant leaving Yvonne alone on their isolated farm without electricity or telephone. It was another dilemma they had to face in their endless struggle to improve their standard of living and to cover the cost of our education.

His departure was scheduled for January, so Yvonne would have the added challenge of facing a winter alone. Papa left her with an ample supply of firewood, but she still had to haul water from the well and tend to the horses in the barn in the bitter cold and deep snow. Leo knew that Yvonne was resourceful enough to handle just about any situation; nevertheless her isolation left him uneasy, and he asked our neighbours to check on her frequently. The day he left, Mama tried to come to terms with her fate. Darkness fell early and at the frosty window, she turned from the gloom without to the gloom within. Her isolation sat heavy on her as she lit the oil lamp and set the table for one. Still without telephone or electricity and so far away from her neighbours, she had to be one brave lady.

Whenever I visit folks in our old neighbourhood, someone remembers Mama's trips to the village in those days. Her only means of transportation was the team of Clydesdales and a heavy sleigh. Before leaving, Papa had shown her how to properly harness the horses. Her four-foot 11-inch frame was dwarfed by those giants, making it necessary for her to climb on a block of wood in order to slip on the bridles and throw the heavy leather harnesses over their backs. When the horses were properly harnessed, Yvonne had to strap them together, back the team out of the stall and outside to hitch them to the sleigh. Of course she had everything ready, because no sooner were they hooked to the sleigh, than they were poised for flight and she had to jump aboard for blastoff. Because the horses were so high-spirited, within seconds they were off at full gallop, which did not enhance the comfort of the rough ride. Nothing could slow their mad race down the snow-covered road.

Those blue-gray steeds streaking by at breakneck speed with Yvonne hanging on to the reins for dear life, was an awesome sight. As the sleigh rounded the sharp corner and headed down the hill, the neighbors crossed themselves. The only way to stop their frantic pace was to pull them over into a snowdrift, which she did, wherever she intended to pick up or deliver a grocery order for these good folks. Even for those neighbours who couldn't read, she was to check at the post office in case any mail had been left for them by mistake. By the time she reached the village, still seven miles away, the team had worked up such a lather, that Yvonne had to cover them with heavy blankets and tie them up in a lean-to by the general store. (Yes, these still existed in 1953.) There she purchased groceries, then headed to the post office where there lurked the possibility of a letter from her family. Along the way, she picked up the latest tidbit of news and gossip rippling about the neighborhood. These weekly excursions were the highlight of her life, her only link to the outside world, and a refreshing change of pace from the daily chores on the farm.

On her return trip they were on a downward slope for over three miles (5 kilometres) at a frightful speed. With snow flying up onto her glasses, it was hard to see the road ahead to make her deliveries. These were important to a number of families who had no means of transportation in the winter and depended on her in this way. Fortunately there was no traffic on the road, and should anyone have been anywhere in sight, they would have cleared the way for their own survival. When she stopped, she had to explain that the horses needed the exercise because, in Leo's absence, they were idle in the barn six days a week. Folks were no less impressed by the sight of this determined little lady and her galloping steeds. The very thought of such an exploit was enough to daunt the bravest among them.

How does one spend months alone in a little house so far from family and friends? Aware of the limbo in time that her solitude forced upon her, Yvonne seized the moment to brood and ponder, suspended between her yesterdays and the tomorrows with their promise of new beginnings. She devised ways to spend her time productively. With no one else in the house, the place remained tidy, so she had plenty of time to be creative. She was instrumental in setting up a dissident school board in our locality. This protestant school board had the right to collect taxes from all non-catholic property owners, as well as a proportional percentage of taxes from businesses and corporations. That money allowed about a dozen other children from our area to attend the same Protestant school we were attending in Namur and live with us in residence. This move was not a popular one with the establishment, but Yvonne was a determined lady, not easy to reckon with in matters concerning children. She would do all in her power to help the local children get equal opportunities with their peers in the village. To this end she spared no effort, and took on the responsibility of school board secretary-treasurer, working closely with the school inspector from the Department of Education. He was a kind man, and as an interesting footnote, I might add that he handed me my teacher's diploma when I graduated from college many years later.

Before long, the Catholic School Board tried to court her into joining forces with them to include the Protestant children in the village school, but that did not sit well with our small community. Mama had fought long and hard to make those gains and would not give up so readily, especially since we now had the added advantage of a bilingual education. Hence we continued to attend school out of town, a lifestyle we had learned to cope with over the years and one, which, though painful, I have not lived to regret entirely.

Having the ability to roll up her sleeves and take on any task, Yvonne had the tendency to overextend her generosity to the point where her tender heart threatened to break her back. She was occasionally called upon to be anything from a midwife to an undertaker. On one occasion, a good acquaintance died. Her life had passed without distinction and she was an old lady well past everything but tea and knitting. Left alone after her husband's drowning accident, she suffered a deep depression and lost the will to live. Yvonne was fetched to wash and prepare the body for the undertaker. As no one else could be persuaded to go near the place, Mama took it upon herself to perform this duty as a last gesture of kindness for these good folks. They were among the families for whom she had run errands with horses and sleigh. Their empty house by the lake left our community with a deep sense of loss.

Winter could be long and gloomy in the solitude of her little cottage, and the snow ghost which danced across that windswept country in the dim light of winter did nothing to pacify her growing concerns. Surrounded by the white immobility of a frozen world, Yvonne refused to focus on her loneliness; instead she undertook to assemble and stitch patchwork quilts. The old tunes she hummed helped to unburden her grieving heart as the antique sewing machine whirred away the hours. She sat by the window where the afternoon sun poured in like butter bringing cheer to these menial tasks, the repeated, dependable activities that anchored her days, giving a sense of worth to her work. Yvonne refused to indulge in self-pity and, instead, made the most of the little she had to bless others. Even with her very limited means, she was able to touch the bruised spirits and wounded lives of others in that community. It was her way of battling loneliness while hopelessness tugged at her soul.

Goose Bumps

Courage is fear that has said its prayers.

Many people wondered how Yvonne could live alone without fear. She often told us that she felt quite safe within the four walls of the house, but she did not relish being outside at night because she was afraid of wild animals. The thought of someone breaking into the house never occurred to her, perhaps because she did not feel that she had enemies.

One night, as she was walking home from a neighbor's house, the brooding darkness was gathering fast. The moon smiled a thin smile on a deserted landscape, and a strong wind threatened to extinguish her flickering lantern. Feeling uneasy, she accelerated her pace towards the woods just as a gust of wind blew out the flame. Panic-stricken, she broke into a run. The path's black shadow cut a wound through the tall grass of the surrounding meadow, outlining it in the dim moonlight. As she stopped to catch her breath, the chill breeze sent cloud fragments scurrying across the face of the moon and the darkness thickened. The night grew dark as death and began to thunder to the voice of the rising wind when a screech owl hooted in the distance. The woods stood before her and she felt the inky blackness swallow her as she crept forward. Suddenly, some 50 feet ahead, four eyes appeared shining in the darkness. She stood petrified, unable to move, her heart drumming in her chest. When the moon came out from behind a cloud, she recognized two magnificent deer, staring at her. They turned tail and disappeared into the night, but she had to wait for her pounding heart to behave before she could move on. As she crested the steep hill, the barn loomed dark and silent like a sentinel in the night. In the safety of the house, Yvonne bullied the dying embers into a roaring fire that soon warmed the room and soothed her spirit. The old wind-up clock by the bed-side ticked a heartbeat into the silence of the little cottage. The next morning, the lamp, still burning, flared pale in the gray light of dawn. Her fright had been very real and it took many weeks before she could be persuaded to walk along that wooded road again at night.

On another evening, Yvonne noticed tattered, soot-colored clouds scurrying by the setting sun. An aggressive wind whipped up, rattling the windows and howling around the stovepipe, and she wondered what trouble was brewing beyond the horizon. The brooding darkness was gathering fast when she noticed that a big window had blown open in Papa's workshop. If she did not secure it, it would smash. She pulled her coat tightly around her and anchored her hat. As she pushed open the door, the wind seemed to be lying in ambush, for it yanked the handle out of her hand and sent the door crashing against the wall. It grabbed her hat and sent it flying into the chaos. In the jaws of the wind, she struggled across the garden to cover the 100 metres in the semi-darkness, clinging tightly to her jacket. Mission accomplished, she ran back towards the house with her heart in her throat. Just before she reached the safety of the porch, a thundering noise pounced from nowhere and crashed close behind her, rumbling in hot pursuit. It sounded like the devil himself was after her. Breathless, she barely cleared the door in time to see a large oil drum rolling across the concrete porch to disappear down the hill into the windy blackness. Her heart pounding, she closed the door securely, perhaps in an attempt to lock out the wind and all its mischief. All night long the screaming wind haunted her sleep, and the next morning, she heard on the radio that the tail end of a hurricane had struck that area. Fortunately the damage was minimal and she had another amusing story to share with us in her next letter.

One night in early June, when Yvonne was alone, she was awakened from a sound sleep by a noise outside her window. It was the silence of the night into which an alien footstep screams its arrival. The spider of thought began weaving a web of fear through her brain as she strained her ears. She had distinctly heard steps on the porch, but from her window she could see nothing but blackness. Over the ridge, in the western sky, a sick-looking moon rested in a bed of clouds. Feeling vulnerable in her isolation, she listened again and, sure enough, someone was walking close to her door. Wondering if a neighbor had come seeking help, she called out from the upstairs window; but there was no answer. This was not normal. She found the matches and lit the oil lamp, then made for the rifle that shared a home with an old umbrella in the upstairs closet. As she loaded the weapon, she was startled by the moving shadow thrown on the wall by the flickering lamp. Undeterred, she marched back to the window and yelled, "Whoever you are, you had better leave because I have a gun and I intend to use it!" At that she blasted a shot into the air. She hadn't quite recovered when she heard a horse galloping away into the night. Feeling somewhat sheepish, she put away her weapon and returned to bed, chuckling to herself. Her assailant had been the neighbor's horse seeking shelter on her porch. Poor creature. Each had been the victim of circumstances.

Marooned in silence, she gazed into the star-lit velvet blackness outside her window. Where the clouds had ragged apart, the sky reached back beyond the stars to a deep blackness that stretched back, it seemed, to the beginning of time. As she closed her eyes, Yvonne rested in the knowledge that her little house was wrapped in the arms of the One who holds the heavens and silently displays His power to all who care to look. She was reminded of the scripture verse, "The Eternel God is thy refuge and underneath are the everlasting arms."

The Smoking Gun

I will say of the Lord,
"He is my refuge and my fortress,
my God, in whom I trust." (Psalms 91:2)

We left Mama at the homestead for another semester at school while Papa was away on his third contract on the D.E.W. line in the Arctic." Summer stretched into October that year, shedding its warmth and gladness far into the North Country. Even as the days shortened, the woods were warm with the color of maple and sumac blazing red their final triumph to the world. The beech and oak shed an amber and yellow loveliness across the hills. Vagrant leaves fell like silent sunny rain, in the golden light of the rising sun. These were the autumn days when the wind tugs at your smile and the sun can still warm your very soul. The loveliness stabbed the ache deep in Yvonne's heart, accentuating her loneliness for there was no one to share it with. As she sat meditating on the porch, sipping her morning coffee, Yvonne understood that day by day, year by year, life goes on till time itself is lost in the great ocean of eternity. She was learning from the scriptures that it is God Himself who guides people with unerring wisdom through all the perplexing paths of life, and will bring us all safely home at last.

Because the business of living always calls us out of our brooding dreams, Yvonne rose to meet the challenges of another day. The only sounds in the house were the muted crackle of the fire in the stove and the soft purring of the kettle. With tear-filled eyes she stared at the clock. Slowly the numbers swam into view. It was only 8 o'clock. She was aware of the turbulence that throbbed within her breast, the restlessness in her heart, begging her to give it proper notice. She tried to suppress it but it elbowed its way forward. She knew she must search her soul for answers. What did God expect of her? She felt like one who dwells in the shades of time with the light of eternity on her brow. So many questions remained unanswered, yet she willed her confused mind back to the present and the task at hand. It was as if time had stopped, but life went on in muted misery as her emotions were numbed by the reality of her situation and the approaching winter she might have to face alone.

In the weeks that followed, Mama looked after our neighbour, Mr. Moon's dog, Daisy. The owner was spending time in Montreal and had left his pet cocker spaniel with Mama for company, company she would gladly have dispensed with. She had obliged to help the old man, but a dog that barks in the middle of the night was not her idea of company. Things were bearable until the day the little bitch came into heat. Male dogs she had never seen before seemed to come out of the woodwork. Daisy was immediately confined to the house with no chance of parole. That helped to discourage her suitors, until one very determined hound began to feverishly dig up Mama's flowerbed. When she attempted to scare away the offending pooch, it turned on her with bared teeth. Frightened, Yvonne grabbed her .22 caliber rifle and fired in its direction with the intention to kill. Being a poor shot, however, she only wounded the culprit who limped home with a bullet in its hind leg.

The owner, a Mr. Scholtz, who lived about a mile away, had heard a shot from that direction and suspected its origin. The angry man was a former Nazi of impressive stature, so when Mama spotted him marching up the hill, she took the gun and promptly hid it in the cellar. That man roared into the house almost knocking her door down, and sniffing around the room, he demanded to see her gun. Feeling terribly intimated, Mama played dumb and watched him search her house like the SS in Hitler's army. He insisted that she had shot his hound and that he would prove it. Fortunately he did not find the wretched weapon and stormed out in the same manner he had arrived.

Thankful that he had not discovered the object of his search, which she strongly suspected he might have used to shoot her, poor Mama dropped into a chair in a heap trying

The Smoking Gun

to tame the pounding of her runaway heart. Never before had she felt so vulnerable in her own home. That incident left her with the abiding fear that he might return at any time to get even. Living so far from her neighbours and without a telephone, how could she possibly defend herself? She went to bed that night with nothing settled but with the conviction of having blundered once again. From that day Mama locked her door at night and decided that, unless she became a better shot, she should avoid using a gun to solve her problems.

As a footnote I shall add the following relevant story. That man's wife was a very dear friend of Mama's and they occasionally confided in each other in broken English over a cup of tea. The woman was emotionally abused in an unhappy marriage. When life became impossible, she would climb the hill and shed tears of anger and distress in our little kitchen. She proudly showed us the pictures of her grandchildren in East Germany, wishing she could visit her daughter. With that goal in mind, she managed to find work in a small inn nearby and secretly saved enough money over several years to visit her family in Europe. One day her husband discovered her stash. He accused her of plotting behind his back and took her money, and with it, her lifelong dream and only hope of escaping from that living hell. A week later, that man found his wife hanging in the barn with a note in her apron pocket. In desperation, she had found a way of escape and left him to deal with his conscience in a large empty house. I still regret not knowing the extent of her suffering in time to help, because this happened long after we had moved away from the area.

One Great Heart

I do not ask for mighty words
To leave the crowd impressed;
Lord, grant my life may ring so true,
My neighbors may be blessed.

When stretched to her full height, Yvonne stood one inch short of five feet (1m 50cm), but she was a great lady. Mama had gained extra weight with her first pregnancy, probably due to gestational diabetes, and was never able to shed those pounds. This remained a real struggle throughout her life. We did not notice the extra weight; her chubby appearance made her all the more endearing to us. She was warm and cuddly like a soft pillow with arms that wrapped around us like a safety belt. For those who cared to look, it was clear that her heart of wondrous sympathy beat in her face.

In spite of her extra pounds, Yvonne was able to sweep everyone along on the coattails of her energy. When she set out to tackle a task, nothing could stop her. In the mid-fifties, the minister of the parish where we attended school decided to build a church in our home community. With Yvonne at the helm, this project would materialize. She rolled up her sleeves and, involving her neighbors, she organized a summer bazaar. That initial fund-raiser would launch the building project. Once the hole for the foundation had been dug, a number of young folk with Lizette and I grabbed shovels and dug a trench for the footing on which cement blocks would be laid as the foundation of the future chapel. Other events followed, and the church was completed in time for a Christmas service the following year. That little concrete-block building stands today as a testament to one determined lady, who refused to be daunted by any challenge. To make certain that all the children of poor families had Christmas presents,

Yvonne wrote to the Salvation Army and received a large box of toys and goodies, which were distributed to a happy crowd at the church

In all circumstances, Yvonne took the necessary initiative to get the ball rolling and move the obstacles that stood in her way. She firmly believed that, even if you are on the right track, you might get run over if you just sit there. She had learned early in her life that God gave us two ends, one to think with and one to sit on. Our success depends on the one we use most; heads we win, tails we lose. She was never satisfied until her ideas galvanized into action and ultimately produced concrete results.

There was plenty of work to do to improve conditions when we consider that Quebec women did not obtain the right to vote until 1940. A good friend who is a retired teacher shared with me her personal experience. When she married in 1944, she had to quit her teaching job. According to the dictates of the Roman Catholic Church, a married woman was not permitted to work outside her home. Her job was to cater to the needs of her husband and produce babies. In 1952, with the crying shortage of teachers, the school board trustees had to give in and she was called back to work, a career she pursued for the next twenty years.

It was men who ruled the world and they made such a sorry mess of it that I have often wondered at the progress that could have been made in Canada, had we ever elected to parliament women of such caliber. Gutsy determination coupled with energy and integrity would certainly have kept our country debt-free and economically much stronger, because such women did not stoop to play the political game. They were visionaries with a practical touch, capable of running a household on a shoestring. What glorious achievements they could have accomplished with the necessary means! What an inspiration they might have been to the political leaders of the day, had the latter taken the trouble to listen to their common sense wisdom!

Papa

Do you love life? Then do not squander time,
because that's the stuff life is made of.

One day when Papa was away in Frobisher Bay on Baffin Island, I asked Mama to tell me more about his childhood. It was that time of day when the trees reached out and touched the places where the sky came down red, the time when we sat together to share stories. Papa had always seemed reluctant to talk about his family; but as the story unfolded, I gained a new sense of respect and admiration for my father.

It all began in 1906. When she was only 15 Marianne married Eugene, a man twice her age. They were very much in love and he spoiled her like a princess. One year later, Leo was born to a 16-year-old mother. As the new baby became the object of her husband's affection, the young mother felt cheated and resented the child. She never displayed much love for him, even as a toddler. The following year, this teen-age mom was further weighed down with a baby daughter. The honeymoon was only a memory and the chores of motherhood took over her life.

When Leo was four, tragedy struck the little family. His father fell into a dry well and died of his injuries, leaving a 20-year-old widow with two toddlers. As there was no social safety net for widows in 1911, Marianne had to be resourceful. Initially, she returned home to her family, but then she had to provide for her children. The young mother took her little ones with her to work in a shanty, a loggers' winter camp deep in the woods. She cooked and baked bread, cleaned and scrubbed for 40 men in that remote location. The 16-hour days in the log cabin were exhausting for the young mother, but the cold proved too much for Leo's five-year-old sister Mary. She died of pneumonia that first winter in the shanty.

The young widow then married a kind man who fathered

a third child. When this second husband became ill with tuberculosis and needed treatment, Marianne had to work in a restaurant several miles away during the summer months. At that time Leo, who was seven, was left alone at home with the responsibility of looking after his six-month-old baby brother every day for the whole summer while his mother was at work. The following summers, Leo had to pick wild raspberries to sell to tourists in order to pay for flour and sugar for the winter months and to buy his shoes for school. He was not allowed to eat the berries as they brought a coveted ten cents a pound.

Teachers in those days threatened to remove one end of whoever dared to question their authority. One day Leo was called to the front of the class for a beating with the stick. When he pulled his hand away, the full force of the stick struck and split the teacher's toe, which increased her fury. He did not wait around for the repercussions, but took off like the wind. He felt that he wasn't suited to the classroom and he had only had three winters in school when he quit and went to work in the shanties as an errand boy. His responsibilities included hauling water and wood for the cook, as well as feeding and watering the horses, preparing the kindling, shoveling snow, sweeping the floor and anything else the loggers could avoid doing.

Every morning, the cook wakened Leo before anyone else to feed the horses in the little barn. One such morning, the dim light of his lantern revealed that there was a hole in the lid of the oat barrel and rats had found their way inside. The ten-year-old was afraid of rats, but too proud to admit it to the men lest he be called a sissy. He was facing a serious dilemma. Leo pondered the situation and walked back to the camp, silently picked up the cat, and returned to the barn. He lifted the lid of the wooden barrel, dropped the cat in, and replaced the lid. The result was instant. For those trapped inside, there was no escape. Ear-piercing squeals were followed by silence, then a soft "meow". The frightened boy lifted the lid, pulled out several dead rodents, and proceeded to feed the horses. The cat had its meals lined up for the day as well. Every morning the same ritual was followed without a word to anyone. When the sun rose, and the men set out full of flapjacks and molasses for the woods, the boy's long day was already an hour older.

Surrounded by rough characters, Leo considered himself a man and learned to cuss and smoke at the tender age of ten. As bit by bit, I ferreted out this sad story, I realized that my father had been robbed of his childhood. Even as a pre-schooler, he had been burdened with adult responsibilities. It was a wonder to me that he had survived these many hardships unscathed.

"When your Papa was 17," Mama continued, "his mother left with his young brother, and was never heard from again. Her son was working on the railroad at the time, and did everything he could to locate her, but without success. That was over 30 years ago, and your Papa believes that she may have died since, though he feels no less rejected and cheated by this event." There was no mistaking the tone of resentment in Mama's voice as she related that part of his tragic story, for she could not comprehend a mother abandoning her own son in this way.

At 19, your father was working for the CPR, building a railway in Ontario. He was part of a work crew that dynamited rocks and shoveled coal, much like slaves of long ago. One day as he reflected on his life, he concluded that he was not much better than a workhorse, toiling for his keep from sunup to sundown. What little he had learned in school, he had long forgotten and he was almost completely illiterate. Feeling quite discouraged, he confided in a friend how defeated he felt in his situation. That man informed him that there was a way out of his predicament. Leo would be able to learn by taking a correspondence course. "I'll help you get started and you will succeed," assured his friend. It was with guts and determination that your Papa did just that. After a ten-hour day of hard labor, he studied long into the night, so avid was his passion for learning. On Sundays, while the rest of the guys went out for a good time, he learned to read English, and picked up a trade, which he is using now in Frobisher Bay. His knowledge of English has been a tremendous asset in helping him to expand his horizons.

So that was why he was such an avid reader. He practically devoured the farm magazines and all those publications my uncle brought with him in the summer. The hard life of a homesteader is not conducive to scholarly pursuits, but daily reading helped to resurrect and grow the learning that had been buried under the accumulated clutter of the years. It was only in the winged freedom of his reading that he found release from the daily grind and dark despair of poverty. It became clear to me why Papa put so much emphasis on our education, when other folk did not think it was so important. I saw my father in a different light. He had become a real hero to me, and though he was a man of small stature, I thought he stood head and shoulders above everyone else. Through hard work and perseverance, Leo had earned a reputation as a man of integrity and determination, another anonymous builder of our great country.

As a preschooler, I would slip up onto Papa's lap unnoticed and listen to adult conversation, aware of the battles they were fighting in the name of freedom. From my vantage point, I was conscious of his genuine love for us. When Papa smiled, his eyes twinkled, but when lightning began to flicker under his eyebrows, we wanted to wilt in our tracks. Hanging by the kitchen sink was a heavy leather strap for sharpening his straight razor. I was still a very little girl when I discovered another purpose for that instrument. In an effort to tame my quick temper, Papa used it to dust me off more often than I like to admit. The strap hurt my pride as much as it hurt my rear end because I very clearly remember climbing the steps to be at eye-level with Papa, and shaking my index finger, how I gave him a royal scolding for spanking me. His abrupt exit from the house left me confused and it was much later that Mama explained that he didn't want me to see him laughing at my fiery temper. It was obvious that I had inherited his fighting spirit. I am now ready to admit that in the long term, the "heat for the seat" policy was not detrimental to my health.

As we grew up and tried to impress Papa with our knowledge, he listened patiently and said little. Now and then he replied, "Of course I am not young enough to know everything." By observing him, I discovered the wisdom of experience and understood that those who think they know everything have much to learn. Papa had done most of his learning in the school of experience. He carried no letters after his name but oh, the things I learned at his side. He attempted to teach us basic values of integrity with simple proverbs such as: "Don't judge a man until you have walked a mile in his shoes". "Mind your speech so that you wouldn't be ashamed to sell the family parrot to the town gossip". He often reminded us to complete a task we had started with the words: "Remember that 'tomorrow' is today's greatest labor-saving device". He hated lies and expected his children to speak the truth. "Falsehoods", he claimed, "are termites in the trunk of the family tree". More than once I heard Papa quietly remind me that "smart people speak from experience, whereas smarter people, from experience do not speak".

"The distance traveled reveals the strength of the horse; as the course of events tests the heart of the man", says a Chinese adage. Looking back, I now realize that in the midst of poverty, Papa had given us a home where respect was the cornerstone, integrity the foundation, and with enough laughter at times to raise the roof. Papa taught me that excellence is the real reward for work, and not the elusive dollar. He liked to remind us that the road to riches is always under construction. Surely the heart of every child beats to the rhythm of a father's love, and we were indeed made to feel that in our house, "children are a poor man's riches".

Eugene Caya and
Marianne Greve, 1906.

Leonard Yergeau and
Marianne with son, Henri,
circa 1924.

Two-year-old Leo, 1909.

A CNR steam locomotive in the 1920s.

Leo (right) amateur boxer,
circa 1930.

Building the CNR near
Paris, Ontario.

Leo's first car, a DeSoto, in 1929.

Our home until 1957.

The barn, built circa 1941.

No Place Like Home

Home – the father's kingdom, the mother's world, and the child's paradise.

When I was growing up, our house was a very humble dwelling built high on the hillside and offering a panoramic view of the surrounding country. It had undergone a number of improvements over the years. Papa had filled the walls with wood shavings by way of insulation. He had put in some new windows and wrapped the outside walls in a covering of red imitation brick tarpaper to keep out the wind. He had poured a concrete chimney at the back to replace the one that had fallen in a windstorm. The corrugated metal roof extended over the front porch, providing shade and shelter over a concrete floor which ran the length of the house. This was a popular refuge in summer when Mama was baking bread and the wood stove made the kitchen unbearably hot.

The view of the garden where the roses spilled their fragrance on the cool night air, the weathered wood above our heads, the wooden chairs all contrived to lure us outside on summer evenings. The setting carried the fresh scents of the earth and whispered of fresh bread and molasses, a place where tales, which had gained in momentum and fascination, carried us together far away and long ago. These stories were legion and they were often a blend of the comic and the tragic as they described ordinary people, who thus became part of our lives.

Inside, the cottage did not sin by any excess of originality. The first floor served as kitchen, dining room, living room and doubled as my brother's bedroom at night. The walls were painted a soft creamy color with red moldings. The table wore a red and white, checkered oil cloth to match the gingham curtains. The floor was hardwood painted orange with a trap door to the cellar. Papa had built cabinets on the wall adjacent to the sink (which had only a drainpipe). On the wall was a roller towel just above the strap. To the right were the table and chairs, and at the opposite end of the room was the indispensable sewing machine by the window. Against the north wall was the stove, and across the room, the milk separator occupied the space beside Papa's roll-top desk. Yvon's bed was squeezed in a corner next to the sewing machine. Beneath the narrow staircase by the stove, was a space to store firewood and a small closet with shelves for Mama's sewing materials.

The second floor was little more than a large loft divided into two bedrooms, with built-in closets under the roof. It was all very compact, with a double bed on each side and a massive trunk as the only other piece of furniture. That was where Yvonne kept her precious collection of snapshots, letters from her family, quilts and small mementoes of the past. At bedtime, I remember gazing out the window over the valley to the east cloaked in evening haze and at the mountain beyond that always caught the golden light of the setting sun. It was a breathtaking view anytime, but particularly awesome in its October splendour. The only picture on the wall was the outdoor scene framed by that uncurtained window,

In spite of the limited space, we managed to function as well as all pioneer families did back then. An apron of scruffy grass wrapped around the small outhouse at the back. As we had no indoor plumbing, the backyard privy served an all-important function most of the year; but come winter, the old "thunder mug" (chamber pail) took over the indispensable for the family, the lid being as important as the pail for everyone's well-being. Beans held a prominent place in the diet of pioneers, hence the nickname "thunder mug" because it echoed the prevailing winds and became the butt of innumerable jokes, along with the outhouse. My sister as I recall, sensed the call of nature whenever it was time to wash the dishes, and usually returned to the house claiming that she had not heard me calling her. (Of course, it could have happened to me once or twice), but she was the clown in the family and full of pranks. Saturdays were bath-time, when Mama heated gallons of water on the stove and filled a large galvanized tub where each one got a royal scrubbing (whether we thought we needed it or not). There was a pause in that ritual in the summer when we went swimming regularly and managed to escape Mama's rough hand.

When Papa bought our first battery-operated radio, sometime in the 1940's, I was old enough to remember, and to this day, I recall my confusion as I searched for the man talking from the box on the shelf. Papa laughed and said something about a very little man hiding in the radio, which added to my confusion. I was convinced that someone had to be hiding in the wood box. Nowadays children are born surrounded with technology, which they don't question because it is all part of their lives. For a four-year-old back then, it remained a great mystery.

On the property, Papa had built an impressive barn to house the workhorses, cows and chickens. The animals occupied the main floor while the hay and grain were stored upstairs in the vast loft. The half of the barn facing south was the henhouse, bathed in sunshine. The 50-foot length seemed like an acre of concrete floor to sweep clean. Papa talked to his animals in soothing tones and before long, even the wild-eyed Ayrshire cow that was always ready to take to her heels at the drop of a hat, began to settle down. I have recollections of the dim light of a lantern hanging from a ceiling beam. While the horses munched and puffed, they didn't mind if I stood by their manger and rubbed their noses. When the oat boxes were licked clean, the milking done and the lantern taken down, we headed back to the house with two pails of warm, frothy milk. The barn was the only building with running water, because it had been possible to bring a pipe down from the well without blasting bedrock.

There was another building which Papa called his workshop, where he kept his tools and repaired much of the machinery he used. The second floor served to raise baby chicks in the early spring. Since that space remained empty most of the year, my sister and I claimed it for our playhouse, where we let our imaginations run free. During the hot summer days, it was stifling up there with a dusty odour reminiscent of baby chicks like rays of old sunshine. When the heat became oppressive, we moved our toys to the pile of lumber, where we had discovered a shaded space on a platform between the rows of planks. It became our secret hideout. On other days, the spruce grove became a magical spot for make-believe. Left to our imagination, we devised an endless assortment of games, and between fishing, swimming, exploring the meadows and woods, and working in the garden, the days flew by and no one ever complained of boredom or Mama would have fixed that in a hurry.

In the early 50's, Papa built a little summer cottage that served as a guesthouse. It stood on top of the ridge behind the barn and had the best view of the whole property. It boasted two bedrooms and a kitchen with a wood stove. The guests had their own privy by the woods, which we visited occasionally, but every time I went, I was greeted by giant wood spiders that made me quickly forget the reason for my visit. Porcupines sometimes took up residence during our absence, so I became very wary of the place. The garbage heap was only a hole for collecting broken bottles, played out tin cans, curled-up old boots; everything else was burned, composted or reused in an endless variety of creative ways. Nothing was ever wasted at our house.

When I was growing up, these four buildings were surrounded by 20 acres of cleared land hemmed on every side by forest. Our lot was on a hillside of rough terrain, dotted with rocks and boulders on an incline of varying degrees. Beyond the fenced-in garden, rose the stalwart boulders, clothed in green moss. They formed part of a stern-faced rocky cliff that stood guard over the little homestead. The cleared land was partitioned into pastures and hayfields by fences of three strands of heavy barbed wire nailed to rough cedar posts. The pond below the house supplied water for the horses and cows in the pasture and doubled as a skating rink during Christmas vacations when we had the energy to shovel off the snow.

Times were hard even in the late 1940s. We had few toys, but that was no problem because we had the great outdoors, and of course, the vegetable garden. Mama had a knack for convincing us that planting and weeding were exciting jobs, though I suspect that as youngsters, we were probably more of a nuisance than any help. As the garden began to yield its abundance, Mama always sent us to pick fresh vegetables for the table and thanked us for our help. Eventually her strategy helped us to develop a genuine love of the soil. All that time spent in Mama's big garden taught us valuable lessons of satisfaction for hard work and the real joy of growing our food. Mama was not only growing vegetables; she was growing future gardeners. That large fenced-in garden grew between the house and the workshop. I have a vivid memory of my first very own garden. Papa had sectioned off a couple of small plots for my sister and me. We were given seeds and dahlia roots to plant and tend. Patience is seldom a virtue with a four-year-old, so I frequently dug up the soil to check on the progress of my crops. At that rate of digging and pounding, even the weeds struggled to survive my "tender loving care'. My sister's garden fared much better because she simply forgot it was there.

Every season was busy on the homestead, but autumn brought a breath of fresh air to the woods after the oppressive heat of the summer. It also marked the end of the swarms of mosquitoes, black flies and houseflies that waged a constant campaign of harassment against us for months. Papa enjoyed the cool clean days of October in the forest when logging was more bearable. Around 1950, a road, about a mile long, was cleared the length of our property. That made it easier to haul the logs out, but it created a new problem, hunting. Men with red caps and plaid shirts poured in from everywhere, shooting at anything that moved. More than once, Papa barely escaped with his life. One day a bullet grazed his lips leaving a blister. He claimed it missed him by a duck's smile. It followed that the best season for logging became the most dangerous, particularly on weekends.

Those were the days of pigtails and freckles, when tears were smeared across our dirty faces and hours were spent together as a family. Now when everyone gathered after supper, that's when a lot of tales were told. In the summer evenings, we sat on the porch listening to the frogs and the song of the whippoorwill in the cool breeze. Papa whittled with his pocketknife and Mama mended socks or hemmed a dress while they told stories of the old days. Some were funny, some were sad, but all helped us better understand where we came from. During those long-ago summer evenings, our sweaty little bodies snuggled happily together on Mama's lap as we listened to the accounts of Papa's adventures on the railway or in logging camps. Mama related her experiences growing up in a large family and how Grandpapa was the fun of every party with his songs and fiddle. These well-spun tales had traveled down the long ladder of the generations and reached our little homestead, giving us a strong sense of family heritage. Though life was not all heavenly shades of contentment, we felt blessed and safe. We didn't feel the need to go anywhere because we had fun at home. Food was plentiful, thanks to the large garden and plenty of hard work, and the milk was as close as the Ayrshire cow in the barn. Crystal clear water, fresh air, and space to run and play were all we really needed. At night, we had the open sky all speckled with stars above and the haunting song of the Whippoorwill nearby. It was still a clean and fresh country. We were a family and when Mama hugged us or Papa took us on his knees, we felt loved.

The Story of Peter Little

Among the many stories the Mama shared with us was the tale of our American great uncle. It was part of the oral history that was imparted to us those many years ago. Like a tree, every family has roots and it is those roots that give the children a sense of belonging. Mama took pleasure in passing on the stories she had heard from her parents, thus sharing her heritage with us.

When Grandpapa Delphis was a boy, his 14-year-old brother, Pierre, had left home after a severe beating from his dad. He had calmly told his father, "The next time you see me, you will have white hair." True to his word, the determined lad then disappeared without leaving a trace. No one knew where he was nor heard from him again. Delphis had been only four at the time and the years soon eroded the memory of his lost sibling.

Years passed and Delphis married and was raising his family on a well-established farm in Ste-Edwidge de Clifton in the Eastern Townships when a stranger showed up speaking with an accent. They exchanged small talk and then the man asked Delphis if he remembered his brother Pierre. It was then that he realized that the visitor was indeed his lost sibling. By then their aged father had white hair and it was with deep grief that he welcomed back the son he had lost because of his violent temper. Family gatherings followed where Pierre became acquainted with his extended family and shared his story.

As his story unraveled, it revealed a strong and determined character, the stuff of novels. The 14-year-old had crossed the US border and worked as a farm hand wherever he could earn his crust. He began by picking potatoes and then moved on to other jobs traveling west. Eventually he was hired to work in a diner with a bar across from the train station in Minocqua, Wisconsin. Pierre had few expenses and was very frugal with his money. When the owner decided to sell the place, Pierre Petit, who had changed his name to Peter Little, counted his cash and bought the place outright. With a secure income, Peter married Lena Schmidt. Lena ran the restaurant and Peter looked after the bar. The couple had a son, Ernest who married Emma Olson who was of the Lutheran faith. Together they raised one daughter, Karen Little, who in turn married Lloyd Schultz. They had a son, Gary and a daughter, Kathryn.

I had the joy of meeting my cousin, Karen many years ago and have kept in touch with her and her family ever since. That is a brief account of how our family came to have American cousins with the anglicized name "Little" from "Petit" and of the Christian faith like us.

The Neighbours

To live above with those we love,
That will be grace and glory;
To live below with those we know,
Now that's another story.

Papa was a compassionate man, with a soft spot for people less fortunate, because he had been there himself. It was an echo of his own experience and he was ready to share his limited resources with neighbors who seemed disinclined to labor, at least by Papa's standards. One man was like the proverbial doctor who didn't want to leave his office in case someone else called in his absence. The worn seat of his pants explained the cause of that man's poverty. While that man sat in his warm kitchen, his wife and daughters struggled in the deep snow to cut down trees for firewood. Another family lived in a grim-looking hut and when Papa learned that the grandmother was selling skim milk to the family for their baby, he was appalled, and decided to give them a quart of whole milk every day. He also brought logs to that neighbor's sawmill in the summer to provide work. The sawed lumber was loaded onto our wagon, hauled up the hill, and stacked a short distance from the house for future use. In the short term, it became our secret playhouse.

Perhaps it was before the Second World War that a Swiss family moved into our community. These folks were well educated, more like landed gentry than most immigrants in the area. Val possessed a brilliant mind, broadened with her travels, and spoke French fluently. Her fine features and regal bearing gave her a look of nobility. She and Mama became fast friends, which brought a whole new dimension into Yvonne's life. That family had three children, and settled on a woodlot across a lake about a mile from our house.

There was no road to their house. A rowboat in the summer and a sleigh in the winter made travel possible, but in early spring and late fall, the lake became impassible. A mile-long trail through the woods was then their only link with the outside world.

When they had to run errands, the children walked that trail, and one day they saw a bear in the forest. When they arrived home frightened, they related the incident to their father who thought it was funny. Hans was an arrogant man and tended to trivialize such incidents. It was not until the day that a black bear lumbered across his path in the woods that he recognized the danger that threatened his family in their isolation. After the war some pioneers began to turn their faces away from the narrow angle of their declining economy and look forward to the widening perspective of a more promising future. That was the case with these good neighbours. Before many years passed, they moved to a Montreal suburb, where he practiced his trade as a mason and became prosperous. Mama missed her very dear friend, though they continued to correspond for many years.

Down the road from our house lived a veteran of World War I. He looked like he was burdened with several more years than the rest of our neighbors. As in all wars there are few real heroes and much more ugliness, tortured prisoners, murder, burned farms, raped women. After the conflict, soldiers of all political persuasions are left washed up and adrift on a sea of emptiness. War is not their fault but inevitably, memories of all the horror becomes their life's burden, largely unspoken and buried deep within their soul. For those of us who have never experienced combat, our minds remain innocent of the stains of sanctioned murder. It follows that we may fail to comprehend how veterans' lives can unravel. As a result of exposure to chlorine gas in the trenches of Europe, Tom Moon's emotional compass was thrown off course, a deviation that was to increase with age and stress, provoking impetuous fireworks of marital discord. Finally his wife had had enough. He had accused her of carrying another man's baby. She left him to care for their three grown sons and he did not hear from her until the day, seventeen years

The Neighbours

later that she sent him a photo of his daughter's graduation. One day he showed me that yellowed newspaper clipping and his eyes welled with tears. She was the carbon copy of the old man. Maybe that is the reason he took a liking to me and bought me an expensive watch as a graduation gift many years later.

When Papa arrived in the area in 1933, that man lived with his three sons and they became fast friends. By the time I was growing up, his house had burned down, his sons had left home and the old man lived by himself. He was a big man and his shirt was hard put trying to keep the front of him covered and during the winter months, his trousers were thirsty for soapy water. He had become a recluse in an old shack with only one window visible in front and a stovepipe at the back. The door was solid wood and as gray as the rest of the house. Nothing had been done to add warmth or color to its drab interior, and its owner didn't seem to notice as he refused to abandon the comfort of his denial. The only furnishings were a bed, a table and a large wood stove surrounded by four blank walls. My folks looked after him and we occasionally cleaned out that dwelling. On one such mission, we showed serious lack of enthusiasm, so Mama reminded us that people intersect our lives at inconvenient times, but those often prove to be God's appointments. I understood then that we were doing the right thing.

Mama was hesitant to invite him to eat with us because he liked to argue, and was willing to go down with his ship rather than alter his course. When he got his knickers in a twist over some past grievance, Mama tried to steer his thinking to more positive ground with her sparse vocabulary, "It don't make no never mind no more." With her limited knowledge of English, she had difficulty speaking her mind and found these encounters frustrating, yet he was a frequent guest at our table. We understood that he could never totally free himself from his past and struggled with the German presence all around him. Past sorrows, it seemed, had crawled deep into his bones and remained anchored in the depths of his being. Papa took pity on him and often walked down to check on the old fellow if there was no smoke coming from his chimney. Such were the silent sermons Papa preached to us as we were growing up, and they had a powerful impact on my life. He once told me that he'd rather see than hear a sermon any day and I tend to agree with him. Unlike the many folks who are content to put away much of their Christianity with their Sunday clothes, Papa's life reminded me of the proverb that says: "Train up a child in the way he should go, but be sure you go that way yourself." Papa did much more than articulate those principles, he modeled them for us.

We got along well with most of our neighbors, but occasional problems arose. To put things into perspective, we have to keep in mind that these were tough folks made brittle by poverty and neglect. One summer Papa's truck was always running low on gas for no apparent reason. Then one day a friend commented on the fact that a young fellow in the area who was out of work, was constantly on the road. "I can't figure out how he can afford the gas to drive around so much." Papa became suspicious and waited in ambush one night near the truck and, sure enough, caught him red-handed siphoning gas. He somehow kept his temper in check and only threatened to make hash out of that thief if he ever caught him anywhere near his property again. That somehow made that man less fond of Papa. That guy was very fortunate to have escaped Papa's fists because he would have left the scene a very different man.

Very early on a frosty October morning, Leo drove to the village on business. When he came to the fork two miles down the road, he decided to turn left. He hadn't driven along that road lately so he started climbing the winding road through a scenic land in its glorious autumn dress. As he drank in the loveliness, he noticed some interesting woodwork on a garage door. He knew the owner and that the property was used only on weekends, so he steered his truck into the driveway to have a closer look.

As he walked around examining the new façade, he heard a noise coming from the garage. "Is anybody in there?" he called. With his ear to the door he thought he perceived what sounded like sobbing, so he turned the handle and peered inside. There by the workbench was the owner bleeding pro-fusely. The man had just slit his wrists in an attempt to take his own life because his wife had left him for another man. In an effort to console him, Papa assured his friend that, in his case, it was a blessing in disguise. The woman he loved was not worthy of him. As Papa bandaged his arms, he advised the man to accept his freedom and start a new life. "You are young and a whole future lies before you." He then proceeded to drive the victim to the doctor's for treatment.

When all was said and done, the day was still young and Papa realized that God had orchestrated his schedule in a most extraordinary way, allowing him to save a life. It was a humbling experience. Two years passed before we received a Christmas card from that man with a snapshot of his new wife and baby. Inside was a note expressing his gratitude for Papa's timely rescue and words of comfort when his world had fallen apart. God's ways are not our ways and it some-times takes extraordinary circumstances to remind us of His amazing love.

Papa's World

Those who do something and fail are infinitely
better than those who do nothing and succeed.

As the years passed, new technology was galloping to the
rescue of loggers. Papa bought an assortment of machinery
in his unrelenting determination to add sinews of steel to
improve logging on the frontier. In the early 1940's, or there-
abouts, he acquired a gas engine on two wheels, that was
pulled by a horse through the woods It was a noisy contraption that moved the six-foot-long saw back and forth to cut
the tree trunks and fell the trees. It replaced two men and
made a funny chugging noise like a small locomotive. We
called it the 'Whit' because that was the name of the manu-
facturer.

Quebec was slowly changing. In 1941 there were fewer
than 6000 farm tractors in the province. By 1961, that number had increased tenfold to over 60,000. After 1945 more
that 9,500 kilometres of power lines were rolled out, covering the land like a spider web suspended by thousands
of wooden crosses along the roads. The oil lamps were ex-
tinguished, iceboxes discarded and replaced by refrigera-
tors. By the 1960's, milking machines and refrigerated bulk
tanks allowed the dairy herds to expand and Quebec families
counted fewer children. The world was changing at an alarming rate.

To keep pace with the growing mechanization of the world
around, Leo replaced that machine with the first chainsaw in
the area. I was there when that marvelous invention found its
way to our house sometime in the late 1940's. Papa opened
the box with caution and appeared to caress the silver-gray
monster. It was a male thing, and males bond quickly with
machines. It looked like Papa had taken his vows, as eagerness swirled around him with the gas fumes and the roar of
the motor. The contraption was a dinosaur by today's standards, but it was a breakthrough back then, a promise to
lighten his workload. Little did he know that just carrying

the 35-pound machine would bring little relief at the end of a long day in the forest, especially when it revealed a mind of its own. As I recall, that chainsaw had the occasional conniption fit, snorted loudly and had a fainting spell. It was all part of the evolution of logging half a century ago.

With limited resources, most of the machinery that made its way to our homestead had had a previous life and was vulnerable to frequent breakdowns. Fortunately, Papa was a brilliant mechanic and could improvise any number of repairs to keep things running. I have vivid memories of so many old vehicles in varying stages of dissection. One day it might be the old truck yawning and surveying its innards all vomited on the ground in a kind of sorted mess. With a limited supply of tools and an abundance of cuss words, the engine was pieced back together to extend its life.

All these improvements, however, translated into very little comfort for Yvonne's daily needs, because the time saved by the machinery was generally invested in maintenance and repairs, along with much of the extra cash. The house changed very little over the years, as did Yvonne's wardrobe. Since she did not drive the truck, she was much more housebound than Papa and consequently suffered occasional bouts of "cabin fever". Her solution to loneliness was to keep busy, and she managed better than anyone I ever met in her circumstances. Weeks went by and months melted into years, and I never heard Mama complain of boredom. Where she lacked the resources, she used her creativity and developed new skills that served her well and blessed our entire family.

In the early years, Papa had a dog. She was an Alsatian, a small version of the German shepherd, and her name was Puppy. She was a devoted friend and as smart as a whip. When Yvon was born, Puppy became his personal bodyguard, and no stranger could approach the cradle. She also became a great playmate for the toddler as he grew up. One day, Puppy was in the woods with Leo and wanted to go home, so she took Leo's mittens from a stump and hid them in the snow. Leo searched high and low for them, and then turned to the dog and demanded that she find the lost mittens. To his amazement, Puppy wandered off, dug them up

Papa's World

and sheepishly deposited them at Leo's feet. He accepted her offering with a look of exasperated amusement.

Another day Leo had crossed the lake on the ice with the team of horses to deliver wood to their neighbors. It was late in the season and Yvonne was concerned for his safety. When he had not returned by nightfall, she panicked. She tied a note to Puppy's collar and sent her in search of her master. The dog was reluctant to leave because Leo had told her to stay home that day and she was not about to disobey orders. Eventually, however, she trotted off into the embracing blackness of the night and followed his trail all the way to that house beyond the lake and barked her arrival. Leo guessed the reason for her presence before reading the note and returned home immediately. Mama said that it was better than sending smoke signals in the dark. It was a sad day when Puppy died, and though I was very young, I remember the spot where Papa buried her. We all mourned her absence, and in an attempt to soothe our pain, we retold all the clever things she had done in the past.

Papa always worked with horses. The team I remember were gray Clydesdales named Bee and Queen, names that may have been inspired by the beehives on the farm. When hitched to the hay wagon, they stirred restlessly, shifting back and forth, tossing their heads and swishing their tails. The jingling of the harnesses were a familiar and comforting sound associated with the warm horsy aroma. How well I remember those magnificent horses throwing themselves against their collars and straining to pull the heavy logs through the woods. It seemed that there was never anything beyond their strength. One day a massive bulldozer had sunk into the quagmire by the lake. There was no machinery powerful enough within miles to pull it out. Papa hitched his team and, using pulleys and steel cables, he surprised the skeptical operator by pulling out the sinking mastodon. In the woods, Papa seldom held the reins; he simply called orders, Gee! Haw! Whoa! and the horses obeyed from a distance. During the summer, tails swished as the horses fed their way across the pasture, running to greet us when we walked by the fence. When we scratched their ears and spoke softly, their liquid brown eyes seemed to understand. Those beautiful animals were very much a part of our family.

Because milk, butter and cream were staples in our diet, there were cows on the farm. These animals were generally placid and grazed lazily in the pasture, came in for milking and behaved as all good cows should. Some time during the summer, when a cow came into heat, the dynamics changed radically. That animal suddenly took to her heels and followed every inch of the barbed wire fence seeking an escape route until she spotted a loose post or a missing nail. Mooing loudly, she managed to squeeze her massive body between two strands of barbed wire and make for the woods, where she disappeared in search of a mate. Sometimes it took two days to find the culprit. By then she was a mess, with a ripped and swollen udder, bulging angry eyes and a nasty attitude.

One day Papa caught up with our big Ayrshire, tied a chain to her collar and tried to coax her back to the barn. Just as he prepared to go, something spooked her and she took off like the wind. At the end of that chain, there was a large metal hook dragging on the ground. The hook caught Papa's heel, knocked him down and dragged him on his back half a kilometer over the rough terrain. When he finally got to his feet, bruised and battered, he was fit to turn that cow into hamburger. Another day a cow pushed down a supporting pillar in the stable and it fell on Papa's head. When he came into the house with blood streaming down his face and a serious dint on the top of his crown, we were convinced that he was dying. Those experiences explain Papa's intense dislike of cows.

On a farm, cats are not merely furballs decorating fine furniture and silk cushions. As children, we loved to play with our kittens and dress them in doll's clothes, but they were useful predators earning their keep like any other livestock. As far back as I can remember, we had cats on our homestead. When I was very young, there was a gray tabby that had to be the best hunter we ever had. She brought home, not only mice, but also partridges, young rabbits and weasels. Sometimes she left them on our doorstep as an offering. I remember Mama actually cooking such a partridge, which the cat had laboriously dragged to the house.

When that female cat took up residence in the barn, she intrigued me by her household management. A cat of the preceding litter was delegated to babysit and care for her little ones while she hunted in the nearby fields. She always brought home live prey to teach the baffled kittens hunting skills. Until the ground was covered with snow and all the wee creatures had gone into hibernation, that feline paced the fields and invariably ambled back sporting a large mustache, usually a fat field mouse, but sometimes, another unwary rodent.

I shall never forget the day a young cat stalked a baby weasel. We watched it pounce and...Ouch! What was that? The weasel had caught the cat by the lip and would not let go. A streaking cat disappeared under the porch, swinging an angry weasel, and squealing in pain. When the weasel decided to make its getaway, our terrified kitten knew better than to resume the chase, and the weasel disappeared into the woodpile. The old mama cat caught up with it later and offered it to the defeated hunter. Would you believe that her offended son refused to touch it? He grew up to be a discerning hunter.

Our neighbour had a noisy little dog that persisted in annoying our cat. She appeared to ignore its presence, or just stare at it with disdain, until one day the dog crossed the line. She had a litter of kittens nearby and there was an invisible sign that must have read: "No dogs allowed". Big mistake. Instantly that placid kitty was transformed into a ball of bristling fury, inflicting upon the canine invader the lesson of its life. Never again did he come anywhere in sight of that dignified kitty.

Because cats have a tendency to multiply over the summer, the barn was usually well populated in the fall. Cat food was too expensive, so Papa found a way to feed them, along with strays that might have otherwise perished over the winter. In early December, he usually bought for $10 an old horse that was destined to the graveyard, walked it home, put it down, skinned it and let the carcass freeze in the vacant chicken house. The sale of the hide covered the cost of the animal, and the cats fed on the carcass all winter, a diet supplemented with a little milk. Come spring the cats were smiling as they picked the bones bare, and Papa still had his little helpers to keep the barn rodent free. Some people maintain that there are more ways than one to skin a cat, but in that instance, Papa figured that it was better to skin the horse.

Though he spent his days in the forest, Papa was not a hunter. More than once a frightened deer escaped the woods during the hunting season and stood, trembling in our field. Papa just couldn't find his ammunition before the animal disappeared. We were all suspicious about his fumbling searches for gun and bullets at such times until, one day he articulated his reason for not killing wild animals. He respected all life and particularly the creatures with which he shared the forest. He explained that he butchered the animals he raised on the farm for food. Deer were not in that category. Neither did he approve of snaring rabbits because he claimed it was cruel to cause an animal to suffocate to death.

In spite of his gruff words, Papa had a tender heart and a great deal of respect for the land, the forest and the creatures in it. I learned much from his attitude toward the environment.

Politics

Definition: Poli = many
Tics = blood-sucking parasites

$\mathcal{B}$efore the days of T.V. and general apathy toward government, politicians traveled all over the country to the remotest corners of the province to persuade voters in their favor. These gatherings generally heated up with the rounds of beer and an atmosphere poisoned by unspoken hostility. An old newspaper article recently took me on a long flight on memory's wings, and I was reminded of the trap of prestige, power, money and connections that can stifle one's integrity. Even in the early days of our country, people suspected that the mutton-chop whiskers and handlebar moustaches of those high-ranking politicians had weighed down their brains.

When I was very young, Papa took me along to hear a candidate scheduled for a rare appearance in our village. While the beer was making the rounds, we sat in a prominent spot and waited with anticipation for the show to begin. I heard Papa say, "There is always free cheese in a mousetrap." When the guest arrived, a hush fell over the crowd. The man walked to the platform and, raising a glass of beer by way of a toast to the party, "Ladies and Gentlemen," he began, encompassing the crowd with a sweep of his glass. I watched wide-eyed, expecting great things to happen, but as he sat on stage, dispensing his limited charm, I was aware that the man's long sentences were no more than refined nonsense. He clearly showed symptoms of having a brain that had stopped evolving when there was still a long way to go. When asked clear questions, he obviously had no intellectual superiority to make atonement for himself. I turned to Papa and heard him mumble his familiar quote: "The empty wagon rattles the loudest." The murmuring in the audience grew louder and erupted into a furious battle, the words flying hot and fast. As the shouting increased, I was frightened.

Just then, a fistfight broke out in the crowd behind us. Aware that an angry, unruly crowd is a dangerous animal to keep at bay, we made our exit, and I began to understand the source of much of our troubles. That man simply could find no other way to earn his crust. With plenty of money lubricating its wheels, the nature of power was not about to change. It was dirty politics. Duplessis exerted his power by the muscular arm of the Roman Catholic Church over a submissive people, because religion was a dominating force back then, full of old superstition that stifled progress for decades in our province. Personally, I have never been able to muster any substantial enthusiasm for politicians because of my serious doubts regarding their integrity. The job description of these bureaucrats fell into two categories, the flagrantly dictatorial and the deliberately nebulous. The first was to impress the general public and the second to remain quietly impotent and to keep them from tampering with the ancient customs and the status quo. And I'll never forget Mama's dismay when she realized that even after a new party had come to power, she had to deal with the same obstinate bureaucrats who had tormented her during the previous government. She had never had a very exalted opinion of the virtues of these public servants who liked to call themselves "government officials" at the best of times, but this had to be the straw that broke the proverbial camel's back. It seemed that the party in power was prone to soar to the heights of oratory about its unprecedented achievements, without suffering any real change of heart about the predicament and real needs of these pioneers.

The Padlock

My parents' audacity to send us to a Protestant school put them at odds with the establishment. This was a particularly drastic move in the days of the Duplessis regime in Quebec, when the party in power, the Union Nationale, ruled the province with the iron fist of the Roman Catholic Church hierarchy. Those were the days when the faithful were forbidden to read the Holy Bible. At that time, many facts remained hidden from the people, lest knowledge should cause dissention. A good example is the Ten Commandments. In the church catechism, the second commandment, namely "Thou shalt not make unto thee any graven image..." had been removed to avoid confusion about the proliferation of statues in every church building. The tenth commandment, consequently, had been divided in order to complete the ten laws of God. Much of the truth of scripture could be easily hidden from the worshippers, because mass was still read in Latin. In fact the church of the day, as in all dictatorial regimes, did not favor higher education for the masses. It was the quiet revolution of the sixties that eventually opened people's understanding, and as a result, church attendance dwindled dramatically.

The extreme poverty surrounding us gave my parents the resolve to continue their struggles to improve living conditions for the whole community. Through the mists of prejudice, they were easy targets because their quest for truth and justice led them away from the path of least resistance. Needless to say, their hand in the creation of a dissident English Protestant School Board in our locality did not endear them to the local government in power. Extremism is the politics of despair and our family was labeled revolutionary, heretics and communists. As Papa was not one to whitewash or bloat the truth, he publicly articulated his convictions, and persecution followed.

To add oil to the fire, someone sent Papa a subscription

to a communist publication, "Le Combat". He was not impressed by its content or very happy about receiving it, as he did not approve of or favor communism. In a small village, the cat was soon out of the bag and it most likely became the catalyst that stirred up so much trouble for us. Some politicians of the day may have been "one brick short of a load" as Papa sometimes said, but the bureaucrats displayed deep prejudice against anyone suspected of free thought. Papa must have been blacklisted on page one in their books.

One day, in the mid-40's, there was a loud knock on our door. Mama was alone in the house as Papa was in the woods hauling logs. She was shocked to face two men in police uniforms, who ordered her to step outside. The officer's words were the kind that make impressions on the soul and elevations on the skin. They promptly placed a padlock on the door and informed her that the property was seized, which, translated, meant they were dispossessed. Mama watched in shock as the men walked away, leaving her locked out of her house. She sank down in a heap, sobbing, "Why is God so far away when I need Him?"

When Papa lumbered home in the gathering darkness, he found his Yvonne sitting on a stump in tears. When he had sorted out the events that had unfolded in his absence, he fetched a crowbar, and with a few cuss words, made short work of the padlock. Repeated attempts to sort out the source of that incident led to a dead end. In the constantly shifting sands of politics, it seemed that no one was responsible. It could be said that no snowflake in an avalanche ever feels responsible. The men in uniform never returned and no more was heard of the matter, but intimidation was a common tactic in those days to frighten people into submission. Since most pioneers were at the mercy of the government for such basic needs as roads, it was risky business to speak out against the flagrant abuses of that ugly regime. Today I am proud to testify that among the brave folks who dared were my parents. Though unappreciated at the time, they were among the unsung heroes and the real builders of our great country.

The Move

Don't be afraid to take big steps;
You can't cross a chasm in two small jumps.

By 1957, this perpetual separation was tearing our family apart and we had had enough. As a teen-ager, I had become increasingly unhappy living away from home. A thought occurred to me, a thought I knew I had no business entertaining. My brother had already graduated from high school, and was working in the far north, but my sister and I had to face more of the same. If we threatened to quit school rather than going back, perhaps my parents would consider moving to a town with a high school. Would they take us seriously? We hesitated, knowing that for them, it would mean turning their backs on 24 years of their lives invested in that property.

Considering that as late as 1957, both the hydro and the Bell Telephone Company had not yet discovered our locality, bordered on bizarre. Of course, this was not uncommon in rural Quebec. The local economy was dead and the idea of continuing to live and invest in such a remote and primitive place was questionable. Why not precipitate matters to allow for some family time at home? My sister and I conspired to persuade my parents to do just that. We insisted that we had had enough expatriation and would quit school rather than leave home again.

After much discussion on the matter, Papa decided to move to Lachute, a small town with a population of 10,000 and a good high school. Packing the contents of our house, all the clutter that had been its normal burden for so many years, grieved us deeply. Memories somehow remain anchored in the land and cannot be packed along with the practical stuff. As we filled the boxes, the sights and sounds of my youth crowded thick upon me. Would we ever return to live here? Probably not. What would happen to the buildings, the cleared land, the fences, the flowers, and the breathtaking view from the boulders on the ridge? The years of hard labour invested here somehow made the property far more precious than its monetary value.

As I walked to the outhouse, I realized that we were leaving primitive sanitation for more modern facilities; but the thought did not loosen the knot in my throat. I concluded that grief in childhood is complicated by a patchwork of circumstances. We were heading towards a better life, but in the same breath, it meant leaving behind an important piece of ourselves, a whole lifetime. The only rises on the endless sea of "life in an institution" had been our visits home. Those vacations had made life bearable, and now we were leaving even that behind. My discomfort was aggravated by the fact that I had somehow contributed to precipitate the move and cause this upheaval. It gave us all a sense of insecurity.

I was 15 and I tried to console myself with the thought that "lost opportunities line our highways of good intentions". It was clear that we had to make this move to keep our family together and to lead a normal life; but as this debate tore at my emotions, my spirit was restless. Recollections of bygone days raced through my mind with each box I filled. Near the end of that summer, we were too busy planning the move and packing to continue the regular maintenance. Our garden was visibly in need of attention. The horses had been sold years before and the barn stood empty. The stillness was heavy around me, as disquieting thoughts crisscrossed my mind. Though I was excited to begin a new life, I was reluctant to part with my past. Then, one evening I walked along the great boulders with the setting sun on my shoulders and peace in my heart, the day's confusion melting into the quiet of the evening. It is not to the hasty observer that the land reveals its beauty. It is only to the one who pauses and listens to its many voices, the birds, the insects, the breeze, the deepening tints and colors of the evening burnishing the hills with copper against a crimson sky. I gazed at the wonder of the fleeting day and experienced a delicious sense of warmth. Across the field, a group of birch intermingled with maple

The Move

and balsam blushed in the fading light along the sagging fence. I had the assurance that we were doing the right thing.

The summer had worn most of its life away when Yvon returned from Baffin Island, where he had spent the previous seven months working on the D.E.W. line. He brought back a duffle bag filled with stories of his adventures in that Arctic frontier, enough to entertain us for weeks to come. It was always exciting to have the whole family together around the table, dimly lit by the oil lamp, chatting late into the night.

Papa had arrived in July from Frobisher Bay, Baffin Island, to reluctantly organize the move. Never before had we paid rent, and without a steady income, we would have to settle for very modest accommodations. It felt like a large portion of our lives was being trundled away. We found a two-bedroom flat on the second floor of an older house, where the living room could double as my brother's bedroom. It was totally inadequate for our family, but it was affordable and would have to do until our finances improved.

The week we arrived, Yvon drove Mama and Papa to Montreal to buy new furniture, including a refrigerator, kitchen and living room furniture, and a T.V. set. Such luxuries promised to make life much easier, and Yvonne could hardly believe her good fortune. For the first time in twenty-five years, she had running water in the house, electric lights, indoor plumbing, and a telephone. Of course, the wood stove on the second floor added a new challenge in winter, but nothing compared to the old homestead.

Such a dramatic change in lifestyle brought a different kind of stress to her life. Yvonne was now fifty-three, that time of life when people tend to put on weight. The move from a hundred-acre farm to a small flat was bad timing. It severely reduced her normal level of physical activity, aggravating her weight problem. Within months of the move, she suffered the physical and emotional strain of an added forty pounds. Her thyroid problem was not going to disappear, and with it her self-esteem took a nosedive. Any other person might have suffered a severe depression, but Yvonne was able to pull herself up by her bootstraps to face the challenge of an uncertain future in new surroundings.

Leo had reached the magic age, somewhere between the sought after and the available. With few job opportunities, he took the money he had saved from his work in the far North and bought a woodlot in the vicinity. His plan was to cut pulpwood and haul it with his truck to the paper mill in the neighboring town. That should provide enough income depending on the quota he could obtain. But for Leo, now past 50 and out of practice with the trade, logging was increasingly demanding. He had to build a small barn to house the horse needed to pull the logs out of the woods. That was before the days of clear-cutting. He could sleep in a shack on the property several nights a week to save time and energy on those short winter days. When the snow deepened and the cold intensified, life became brutal again. The labor was not any different; only the setting had changed. Logging had never been a profitable business at the best of times, but with limited quotas, the small income made for a compressed budget. Yvon had enough money saved from his contract in the far north to buy a truck and begin his own business, a transport operation.

One day Papa came home early, pale and visibly disturbed. "You remember that neighbor I told you about who was so abusive to his horses? I warned him more than once about his brutality." I recalled Papa's concern for those animals. "Things must have been even worse than I suspected, because I just witnessed something unbelievable. His horses were outside today by the lake and together they walked out into the deep water, lowered their heads and drowned. They committed suicide before my eyes." Tears welled up as he related the tragedy. "It was their only means of escape from such cruelty. That man is a criminal and deserves to be in jail." He lit a cigarette and I remained speechless. I knew that Papa felt guilty in spite of his repeated attempts to help those poor animals.

For the first time in our lives, my sister and I could ride a school bus to school and return home for supper with the family. What a concept! I remember the high school principal's reaction when he read our report cards from the village school. "We'll see if you can do as well here." Taking his words as a challenge, which had probably been his intention, we determined that day to prove that country folk could perform as well as or better than the privileged class. Perhaps we had not had equal opportunities before but tomorrow held a promise of better things.

The massive brick building was so much larger than our little village school. We would discover that it housed multiple classes for grades one through eleven, and a student population of well over 600. What a pleasant surprise to discover that specialists taught various subjects. The French teacher spoke French and the math and science teachers could answer my questions and clarify any vague concepts. Wow! This had to be easy. My sister, Lizette, chose the secretarial option, which led to a career in office management. I chose the science course with a university degree in mind. We were both in the hands of a very competent staff who inspired their students to standards of excellence. I held my teachers in very high esteem, and to this day, I have not met a principal equal to Fred Royal, a man of competence and distinction. It was in that context that we launched with heart and soul into our studies, Liz in grade nine and I in grade ten. After an initial adjustment, we made new friends, and before we knew it, life was steering us towards new adventures.

Hauling pulp wood
in Lachute, 1957.

Lizette and Yvon
clearing land,
La Minerve, 1955.

Yvon on the
D.E.W. line, site 41
Baffin Island,
1957.

The Answer

Religion can reform;
Only the gospel can transform.

*L*ooking back on our decision to move to that particular town, I realize that it was a wise choice. God has a purpose for all things and a divine plan for each person. Yvonne was no exception. From her youth, through much hardship and suffering, she never doubted God's faithfulness. Though her faith in her own religion had been severely tested, she always believed and trusted in God, and acknowledged Him as the source of every blessing in her life, especially since she had been reading the Bible. She was grateful for the tiniest gifts and comforts that most people would take for granted. Is it not written, "And you shall seek me and find me, when you shall search for me with all your heart."? (Jeremiah 29:13)

It was shortly after our move that we began to attend a small evangelical church, where we heard the good news of the gospel. Everything I had learned in Sunday school and in the classroom about God and the Bible suddenly made sense, and life took on new meaning. It was such a simple message, and yet so profound. I had been taught that pleasing God was a matter of obeying a bunch of do's and don'ts. I discovered that being a Christian is not about rules, but about a relationship with God. The scriptures read: "For it is by grace you have been saved, through faith- and this not from yourselves, it is the gift of God- not by works, so that no one can boast." (Ephesians 2:8,9) And again, "For God so loved the world that he gave his one and only Son, that whoever believes in him shall not perish but have eternal life...Whoever believes in him is not condemned, but whoever does not believe stands condemned already because he has not believed in the name of God's one and only Son." (John 3:16, 18) I had read these verses before but had not realized their true significance.

The Bible is God's message to man, and teaches us that He is holy, and that each of us has a problem we hate to admit. No matter how good we try to be, we fall short of God's standard of perfection. Consequently, our sinful nature, like a huge barrier, separates us from Him. The good news is that God loves us so much that He provided a way for us to have a relationship with Him. He sent Jesus Christ, His only Son, to earth to pay the penalty that we deserved for our sins. He condescended into the prison of a human body to dwell among us. Born in a barn, He lived among the poor, shared the pain of suffering, wept with the grieving, endured affliction, and was counted among sinners, endured the bloody sweat of Gethsemane, was betrayed, crowned and robed in mockery, beaten and pierced. He offered Himself up for our atonement. Jesus lived that perfect sinless life, which none of us can live, and then he took the punishment that we deserve when he was crucified on a cross. He died for our sins and rose again three days later as proof that he had conquered death. Though many hated and rejected Him, Jesus gave his life for our eternal souls. I finally understood that the life that he lived qualified Him for the death that He died, and the death that He died qualifies us for the life that He lived.

My Advocate

I sinned. And straightway, at once, Satan flew
Before the presence of the Most High God,
And made a railing accusation there.
He said, "This soul, this thing of clay and sod,
Has sinned. Tis true that she has named Your
name,
But I demand her death, for You have said,
'The soul that sins shall surely die.'
Shall not Your sentence be fulfilled?
Is justice dead?
Send now this wretched sinner to her doom.
What other thing can righteous Ruler do?"
And thus did he accuse me day and night,
And every word he spoke, O God, was true!
    Then quickly One rose up from God's right hand,
    Before whose glory angels veiled their eyes.
    He spoke, "Each jot and tittle of the law
    Must be fulfilled; the guilty sinner dies!
    But wait – suppose her guilt were all transferred
    To Me, and that I paid her penalty!
    Behold My hands, My side, My feet! One day
    I was made sin for her, and died that she
    Might be presented, faultless, at Your throne!"
    And Satan flew away. Full well he knew
    That he could not prevail against such love,
    For every word my dear Lord spoke was true!
        By Martha Snell Nicholson (adapted)

We learned from the pages of scripture that God offers us His forgiveness as a free gift. There is nothing we can do to earn it, but to admit and recognize our sin and gratefully receive His salvation. It was overwhelming to realize that God loved me so much that He had paid the ultimate price for my salvation. As I examined my life, I saw myself as part of a happy crowd floating down the river of life, laughing and totally oblivious to the great chasm downstream sucking the swift currant over a roaring cataract. I understood that it was impossible for me to reach the safety of the shore by myself. I needed the Savior. I knew that life is the only time allotted to us to respond to the gospel. Because no one can count on tomorrow, I yielded my life to the Lord.

For Yvonne this simple message had been veiled to her prior to that time by the liturgy of formal religion. The Bible was like a mirror. It held up her life and, with vivid flashes, she read the years. When this good news became clear, she had eternity stamped on her heart. So it was with gratitude and joy that Mama accepted Jesus as her Lord and Savior. At last she had met the one who had cared for her in her deepest needs and could set her free from the scars of an abusive religious system. Mama was amazed to realize that all along the path of her life, the Lord had been only a prayer away. The secret lay at the foot of the cross. The fog was lifting and she could discern the face of Jesus on the pages of scripture. Like Job, the ancient patriarch, she could say, "I know that my Redeemer lives, and that in the end He shall stand upon the earth. And after my skin has been destroyed, yet in my flesh I shall see God." (Job 19:25,26)

She understood that it was not one denomination exclusively that held this message, but the pages of scripture. Yvonne had just discovered the all-important message of the Holy Bible, which was still forbidden to all Catholics in Quebec until late in the 20th century. She had been reading the scriptures for years, but she had missed the message of salvation by grace. "Behold! The Lamb of God who takes away the sin of the world!" (John 1:29) What a revelation! What a sense of liberation! Having experienced oppression, one feels the joy of redemption more intensely. It took some time for Mama to come down to ground level, so elated was she to experience this new-found peace and joy. Regardless of circumstances, her life had acquired a new sense of purpose, for she was no longer alone in her struggles. She had found a friend in the person of Jesus, the risen Lord, not a helpless babe in his mother's arms or a dead man on a cross, but the living God. Her great compassion and religious convictions were now woven together to form the fabric of a genuine and living faith.

In her usual persuasive manner, Yvonne launched into a crusade to save the world. No one was safe from the gospel message in her presence, and many a poor soul heaved a sigh of relief when he managed to wriggle out of earshot of her preaching. Had she gone door to door, she might have been a good witness for certain popular cults of the day; but she limited her good will to relatives and friends, many of whom eventually did respond to the claims of the gospel. They also experienced the same peace as Mama did and to this day, remain grateful for her persistence. It was Mama's joy to infect others with a passion for serving the Lord.

In the same little congregation, we made new friends. One lady was about the same age as Mama, and was also called Yvonne. They had much in common and, together shared each other's burdens. With a rich sense of humour, they could so enjoy the present that the past and the future could not put parentheses around it to suffocate it. When God stitches a church family together like a patchwork quilt, the thread that connects is stronger than shared genetics; it is the thread of His divine love. I learned much in the fellowship of that little group of worshippers, not the least of which is the fact that beautiful young people are accidents of nature, whereas beautiful old people are definitely works of art. And in the weeks and months that followed, the Bible teaching contributed much to shaping my character as a teenager.

Tante Yvonne

There isn't much that I can do,
But I can share my bread with you,
And sometimes share a sorrow, too.

There isn't much that I can do,
But I can sit an hour with you,
And I can share a joke with you
And sometimes share reverses too.

There isn't much that I can do,
But I can share my flowers with you,
And I can share my books with you
And sometimes share your burdens too.

There isn't much that I can do,
But I can share my songs with you,
And I can share my mirth with you,
And sometimes come and laugh with you.

There isn't much that I can do,
But I can share my hopes with you,
And I can share my fears with you,
And sometimes shed some tears with you.

There isn't much that I can do,
But I can share my friends with you,
And I can share my life with you
And oftentimes share a prayer with you.
(Author unknown)

Shortly after our move from the homestead, Mama met a kindred spirit by the same name. Their friendship took the edge off Mama's loneliness as she adjusted to her new surroundings. They were roughly the same age, and in time, their friendship deepened and each became the 'confidante' the other needed in their respective circumstances. This is the story of the dear lady we liked to call "Tante Yvonne".

Yvonne had also grown up on a farm with a large family, and had never been touched by extravagance. She had married young and had raised 12 children of her own, also in an isolated community. For many years they had lived beyond the reach of the power and telephone lines. She once confided that for every pregnancy she had suffered from morning sickness for the entire nine months. When I expressed my sincere compassion, realizing that her sickness had totaled nine years, she laughed and assured me that she must have been insane to repeat the same ordeal 12 times. Yet in spite of these trying circumstances, each one of her children was very precious to her.

When we met the family, the youngest child was eleven and Tante Yvonne was already looking after a number of the grandkids. She taught me that children are a lifelong commitment down through the generations. She was in her fifties when her husband lost his job and she found employment cleaning banks and other buildings to pay the bills, all the while struggling with severe bouts of phlebitis in one leg. Through all the hard times and dark valleys, Tante Yvonne saw the funny side of life. As I look back, I recall her smiling face, and am reminded of the words of Victor Hugo, "Laughter is the sun that drives winter from the human face." I saw her cry, but never found her gloomy, because she could laugh through the tears and lift everyone's spirits. She was a very gifted seamstress and a delightful cook. My beautiful wedding cake was her creation. It seemed to me there was nothing she could not do, and much like Mama, no situation she could not handle.

As she grew older, the obstructed blood vessels in her legs caused severe pain and became a life-threatening condition. The doctors decided to amputate her leg. Poor Mama refused to accept this terrible verdict, and just could not imagine her 80-year-old best friend confined to a wheelchair.

Tante Yvonne

She struggled in prayer, and bombarded heaven's gates with her incessant intercessions, but the verdict held and Tante Yvonne lost a leg. When I visited her and shared how Mama had never accepted God's will, and had insisted that God had been unfair with her, Tante Yvonne laughed as she understood this painful setback as a singular act in the grand manuscript of God's drama. She maintained that our Lord, in His wisdom, makes no mistakes. "I know why God allowed me to go through that surgery", she insisted with a twinkle in her eye. "While I was in rehabilitation, I shared the gospel message with many people, sad, lonely, frightened people without hope, and at least eight accepted the Savior into their lives. They left the hospital totally transformed. It was worth losing a leg at my age because, when I get to heaven, I will be given two legs to walk the streets of gold." It was clear to her that her suffering had been accessory to their salvation, and therein was the victory.

Tante Yvonne's faith was practical and planted firmly in the scriptures, which she had learned at her father's knee, a faith that could not be shaken by the winds of adversity. As a footnote, I might add that her father at age 89 was the lay preacher who had explained the gospel to me when I was a teenager. I have no doubt that Yvonne made it to heaven on one leg, another work of art to grace the gallery of God's great masterpieces and on her arrival the angels rejoiced. The celestial bubbly was taken out of the refrigerator, and together with Mama, they are having the time of their lives. No longer will they have to keep the telephone line red hot from overuse.

A Trip Home

Give me a house to call my own,
Family and friends to make it a home,
Love and kindness that never depart,
Enough to fill a thankful heart.

In late autumn in 1957, we drove north to spend a weekend at the old farmhouse. Along the winding road, I was aware
of the signs of a fast-approaching winter. The mountains
were already pulling white shawls around their hunched
shoulders, as the trees stood almost naked; their shredded
garments fluttering at their feet. My thoughts, much like the
flocks of wild geese, winged their way backward in time to
our life on the farm. Out of the blur of the rewind came a
seen from my childhood.

It was 1955 and Papa had just returned from the Arctic
and had been to the village for errands the previous day.
We were all sitting around the kitchen table eating pancakes
with molasses. The sun had pierced the early morning fog
and through the east window, its filtered beams bathed the
little kitchen in yellow light. Papa sat quietly in the old chair
with the worn leather seat. I sensed that something was trou-
bling him, for his face was the colour of emery paper and he
was already lighting a cigarette. It was obvious that he was
in the throws of another battle with government officials. Unable to find the words with which to frame the sentences, he
hesitated, trying hard to remain composed. Finally, crushing
his cigarette butt in the ashtray, he blurted out the words.
"Our property has been posted up for sale in the village. It's
up for grabs." Mama's mouth dropped open, spilling dismay.
We all sat dumbfounded, as the painful memories of past
confrontations with the Duplessis regime crowded in on our
little family.

The same bureaucrats always managed to strangle and
stifle any effort to break the shackles of this infamous re-

gime. Would we never be free? After 20 years, we had not yet qualified to obtain the necessary documents granting us full ownership of the farm. The original papers were obscure and the real intention somehow lurked threateningly among the tangle of "whereas" and "hereafters" that covered several pages of the impressive document. Clearing and cultivating a percentage of the land had been only the first strand in the long tangled skein that had yet to be unraveled, and had left us vulnerable to such abusive treatment and exploitation. Now my parents stood to lose everything they had worked for and into which they had invested two decades of their lives.

Mama carved her mouth into controlled wordlessness and took down the soda box. She always took soda when she had trouble digesting. As anger battled with despair, Papa paced the floor. "Someday...someday..." and the embers of unrest smoldered on. Their determination to save our property became the stuff of nightmares. Again they were taking on the world, and our family was bleeding. We witnessed another flare-up in the perpetual struggle that was the lot of those who dared to challenge the status quo. Desperate times called for bold measures, and letters to various newspapers finally embarrassed those involved into backing down. Months passed before the threat of eviction was lifted and, once again we could relax and call this property our home. That had not been their first such experience. When his original woodlot was not yielding enough wood, in 1940, Leo obtained a second woodlot to support the family. Over a ten-year period, he cleared ten acres of forest to grow hay and oats, and continued logging the timber in winter. Since Leo made no secret of his political allegiance, he became the object of revenge. In 1950, that woodlot with ten years of hard labor was seized and given to a party favorite (l'Union Nationale), and by way of compensation, Leo was awarded $70. In a land where power knows little justice, a homesteader could be exploited at will without recourse. The man who took that land never completed the required conditions nor did he clear another square foot of land. Yet he was quickly awarded the title deed with no hassle. Is it any wonder Leo had grown such a fighting spirit? To add insult to injury, when Papa was still trying to acquire the title deeds to our original property twenty years later, the ministry suggested it be given to a local resident as a second lot. (Exactly what had been denied Leo in 1950.) As a child, I had already taken too many of the cares of life on my young shoulders.

That day as the drive northward continued in silence, I wondered whether we would find a padlock at the gate or new residents occupying our house. Such were the possibilities under that dictatorship, as the government retained part ownership of our property under the strange laws of the "Colonisation". Fortunately, my fears were unfounded. As the truck nosed its way around the last bend in the road, Papa shifted into low gear and nursed his groaning charge up the steep hill and I was comforted to find things as we had left them several weeks earlier.

Papa bullied the fire into showing a little spirit and added some seasoned maple. A fire roaring in the stove had soon warmed not only the little house, but our spirits as well as we sat reminiscing around the kitchen table. Outside, the velvet curtain of night descended early and the wind held its breath as the moon rolled out a golden carpet across the pond. The stars looked like sprinkled silver dust, a million sparkling ships on a vast ocean. That night, memories rushed upon me as, from my bedroom window, I gazed into the vast expanse of the universe, wondering what the future held for our family as well as for this abandoned homestead. Would we find the time to visit often? Would Papa sell the place? I wondered whether the buildings would fall into ruin and disappear like cities of old that have been discovered in recent digs, Future generations might be curious about the primitive equipment they would find in a postmodern world. But sleep cut short my musings. Bright coral fingers of dawn pushed back the curtains of darkness to reveal a glowing, smiling world. The morning sun brought other thoughts of a more practical and immediate nature. A weekend was always too short when home was the setting, so I had to make the most of our brief visit. Somehow, I knew that I had not seen the end of our dear little house.

The following are examples of the countless letters received over the years in response to their repeated efforts to obtain the title deeds to their property.

MINISTÈRE DE LA COLONISATION
PROVINCE DE QUÉBEC
CABINET DU MINISTRE

Québec, le 27 novembre 1951.

Monsieur Léo Caya,
   La Minerve,
      (Labelle).

Re: lot 50/XI - La Minerve.

Cher monsieur,

J'ai bien reçu votre lettre du 20 du courant, par laquelle vous demandez comment il se fait que le nouveau propriétaire, monsieur Yvon Talbot, a payé au Département de la Colonisation la somme de $100. pour valeur des améliorations effectuées par vous sur le lot ci-dessus mentionné, et qu'une somme de $70. seulement vous a été remboursée.

A l'étude du dossier, nous constatons, par le rapport de notre enquêteur spécial, que les améliorations existant sur ce lot lors de l'annulation de cette vente, le 10 mars 1949, s'élevaient à la somme de $100. mais, par la suite, nous avons été informés par le comptable de notre département que vous nous deviez le montant de $30. pour travaux mécanisés. Le fait est que les améliorations qui existaient sur ce lot ont été faites en partie à l'aide des machineries du département, et la part que vous deviez nous rembourser se montait à $30.

C'est la raison pour laquelle vous n'avez reçu que $70. des $100. qui ont été payées au département par monsieur Yvon Talbot.

Votre tout dévoué,
Le ministre,

b/b

J. - D. BE...

Québec, le 10 mai 1974.

Madame Léo Caya,
C. P. No 59,
Lachute, R. R. No 5,
Comté d'Argenteuil.

Re: Le lot 48, rang XI, canton La Minerve.

Madame,

Nous vous référons à la déclaration que vous avez signée en mars dernier relativement à l'obtention des lettres patentes du terrain susmentionné.

D'après un rapport d'inspection qui nous a été produit nous constatons qu'aucune des conditions du billet de location émis à Léo Caya, le 14 juillet 1933, n'est intégralement remplie tout particulièrement aux item 6, 8 et 9.

Dans les circonstances, nous nous voyons dans l'obligation de ne pouvoir donner suite à votre requête et nous nous permettons de vous suggérer de vous départir de ce lot en faveur d'un cultivateur de la région qui pourrait en disposer comme lot d'appoint.

Dans une telle éventualité, vous devrez au préalable solliciter l'autorisation du ministère.

Bien à vous,

Le service de la concession des terres.

Québec, le 29 mai 1974

Madame Léo Caya
C.P. # 59
Lachute, RR # 5
Comté d'Argenteuil
(Québec)

Sujet: lot 48, rang XI, canton La Minerve
(100 acres)

Madame

Je reçois votre lettre du 20 courant et dois vous dire que Messieurs J.-A. Carignan et Henri-Paul Thisdel, respectivement chef et chef adjoint du service de la concession des terres de notre ministère, ont tous deux pris leur retraite en 1973.

Quant aux conditions d'établissement mentionnées sur le billet de location pour permettre l'émission des lettres patentes pour ce lot 48, rang XI, canton de La Minerve, concédé à Léo Caya le 14 juillet 1933, elles sont les suivantes:

Item 6) Il devra, dans les douze mois de la date de la vente, bâtir une maison habitable d'au moins 20 pieds par 24, l'occuper et y résider personnellement et sans interruption de ce moment jusqu'à l'émission des lettres-patentes;

Item 8) A l'expiration de six années, il devra posséder sur le lot une grange d'au moins 20 pieds par 25, et une étable d'au moins 15 pieds par 20; les deux pouvant néanmoins consister en une seule et même bâtisse;

Item 9) Les lettres-patentes ne seront émises

GOUVERNEMENT
DU QUÉBEC

MINISTÈRE
DE L'AGRICULTURE

200-A, CHEMIN STE-FOY
QUÉBEC, QUÉ
G1A 1E4

...../2

Madame Léo Caya .....

que lorsqu'une étendue de terrain, représentant trente pour cents de la superficie du lot, aura été défrichée en un seul bloc et mise en bonne culture. Dix acres, au moins, de la partie en culture doivent être labourées.

Vous constaterez, madame, qu'à la lecture de ces conditions d'établissement mentionnées sur ledit billet de location, le ministère est dans l'impossibilité de vous accorder les lettres patentes que vous sollicitez depuis plusieurs années.

Bien à vous

le chef du service
de la concession des terres

Strangers from the Past

It was shortly after my graduation from high school that Papa received word that his mother was visiting her relatives in, St-Zephyrin, a village in the Eastern Townships. He was totally shocked at the news because he had been certain that his mom had died long ago. He immediately prepared to leave with Mama to find Marianne, whom he had not seen in 35 years. It was a tearful reunion and he brought her back with him to meet his family. We had to wrap our mind around the fact that we now had two grandmothers. It was a new concept and we embraced her warmly and tried to make her feel loved as part of our family. She was happy to make our acquaintance and we had everything to learn about her many years away. It turned out that in 1924 she had traveled north on a train with Oscar Boisvert and her son, Henri to the new mining towns of Rouyn-Noranda and beyond to start a new life in an isolated community. She had no explanation for never contacting her eldest son. Had she not worried about her 17-year-old or what could have happened to him in the years that followed? I am convinced that she had been ashamed of her relationship with Oscar and preferred to keep that a secret. When she returned home, we kept in touch by mail during my years in college. Eventually I was able to visit her house near La Sarre in the Abitibi region of northern Quebec. We celebrated her 70th birthday with her son, Oncle Henri, his wife Tante Palmyra and their daughter Carmen in La Sarre, when I was teaching in Noranda.

One day, at the end of the summer when I was home and preparing to leave town for my first teaching assignment in Noranda in northern Quebec, a stranger came by asking to see Leo. I asked him if he wished to wait for his return but he politely declined and said he would be back soon. I had a strange feeling that I knew this man or that we had met before. When he returned Papa was expecting him wondering what the visitor wanted. Much to our surprise, he introduced himself as Henri, Leo's half-brother whom he had not seen in nearly 40 years. The resemblance was uncanny. No wonder he had seemed so familiar. It was a tearful reunion as the brothers tried to catch up on each other's lives. It turned out that he lived with his family in La Sarre, not far from Noranda, so I gratefully accepted to travel with them the 400 miles to my destination, which gave us plenty of time to become better acquainted. Later I would visit their home and meet the rest of their family and see my Grand-maman Caya who lived nearby.

Strangers from the Past

Papa meets his mother after a
35-year absence.

Karen Little, 1961,
American cousin.

Leola's HS graduation in 1959
with her proud parents.

Leola, Papa and Eileen Bryson,
Macdonald College, 1959.

College

If you wish success in life, make perseverance
your bosom friend, experience your wise counselor,
conscience your older brother,
and hope your guardian genius.
(Joseph Addison)

Two years after our move from the farm, I graduated from high school with honours and planned to attend teachers' college. That summer, I landed my first official paying job, namely looking after a kind old lady who had suffered a stroke. I spent weekdays with her to cook her meals and help her get around, dress and look after her house. She was very pleasant company, but I was glad to spend my weekends at home with the family. What little money I earned, I saved to pay for my college expenses. The rest would have to come from government loans and bursaries and any scholarships I might receive along the way. My budget would be extremely tight.

Autumn was fast approaching and the thought of leaving home brought mixed feelings of excitement and uncertainty. For the first time, my sister and I would be separated, making this goodbye more difficult. Feeling sad, we both took comfort in the possibility that I would return home for the occasional weekend. I was to share a room with a friend who lived in a neighboring town, so we could travel together.

It was September, just before the pages of time turn to loose leaf, when I packed my suitcase and moved into a room on campus. Though financially strapped, Papa dug out a faded wallet from trousers that had seen several winters and handed me a few bills to cover emergencies. I hesitated, knowing that there might be bigger emergencies at home, but he insisted and sent me off with a sparkle of pride in his eyes. Higher education was the inheritance he had hoped to give each one of us. Mama watched as I walked toward the appointments I had made with life, praying for my welfare.

Once the dust had settled, I learned a new way of life: campus life. I had the advantage of living in the women's residence, where the very walls enfolded us in joyous camaraderie. This new life on campus felt like gleaming ice on a pond, shiny and promising, and as I pondered skating on its smooth surface, I wondered. Will it hold? Can I trust its strength? Before long, the days were swallowed up in a busy schedule and I became well-acquainted with the tyranny of the urgent. I was reminded that "tomorrow" can be today's greatest labor-saving device, a trap to be avoided at all cost. Endless lists of books to read, lectures, term papers, exams, teaching experience, all vied for my limited time. In the vast auditorium, as I listened to a procession of lecturers, I felt I could stretch my mind without doing violence to my soul. Learning became an exciting and all-consuming experience. The resources at our disposal cast a sweeping light on the many targets of human curiosity, motivating students to deepen their search for knowledge. I felt that I could drink my fill at this fountain of learning where my thirst for knowledge was being quenched. It was not until I became involved with children in the classroom that I learned the most valuable lessons that I have carried with me all these years. One which I have cherished is the following: "Until a student knows how much you care, he won't care how much you know."

Christmas arrived in a flurry of snow, and I returned home for the holidays with a friend from Trinidad. Many foreign students were unable to travel home for Christmas, and the idea of anyone spending the holidays in residence was unthinkable. Hilary was black and Mama loved her from the start. Because she could not get her tongue around the name "Hilary", Mama chose to call her by her boyfriend's name, Bobby; and the little flat rang with laughter as it was stretched to accommodate one more body. Yvonne had grown up with the philosophy that in her home, there would always be room for one more, and she somehow managed to stretch the space and the budget to suit the occasion. We spent a delightful vacation and a much-needed break from school. Even in those cramped quarters, I luxuriated in the familiar sense of comfort that settled over me like a feathery eiderdown.

The morning after our arrival, our neighbour's five-year-old son came by to say hello. When he spotted Hilary, he stopped short. Never before had he seen a black person, so he sat and stared. When Hilary washed her hands and face before breakfast, he jumped up and checked the water. With a puzzled look on his face, he returned home. That was indeed a great mystery, and Mama winked at Hilary who chuckled with delight. One day, we asked Mama her opinion on "women's lib". She winked and answered with a twinkle in her eye, "You must realize that women who want equality with men lack ambition." We both laughed our approval.

During my years in college, I met a number of colourful characters. Among the people I remember, was a nurse named Mary. She was from Scotland, and when there was a hole in the conversation, she moved in to mend it with her own brand of humour. She assured us that Scots had to be tough folk coming from a land where thorns grow waist-high and trousers had not yet been invented. When someone commented on her well-endowed bosom, she replied, "One who lives in a food paradise, generally puts up a big front."

One evening when the air was heavy with assignment overload, a few girls congregated in her room for a break and a few good laughs. She told us about her uncle who had survived the war, though he had been shot through the chest. "How come you didn't die? She had asked him. His reply, "Me heart was in me throat, Lassie!" That was typical of Mary's brand of humor and her ability to release tension. There was the hilarious story of her attempt to steal strawberries from a farmer's field with a friend one night when she first came to Canada.

"What am I groping for?" she whispered in the dark.

"Just pick little round things," ordered her friend.

"Yuck!"

The little round things Mary picked, she discovered later, were rabbit droppings.

With Mary, I summarized that hearty laughter is a good way to jog internally without having to face the elements.

Then there were the guys from the men's residence across campus. The handsome ones were spoken for and the smart ones were too busy. One fellow reminded me of a rooster who thought the sun had risen to hear him crow. He was tall and arrogant and no one seemed famished for his company, yet he imposed his presence at the most inappropriate times. It was obvious that he lacked the expertise for courting, as he always appeared to want an appointment to have his ego inflated. The girls tried to keep a low profile whenever we spotted him heading in our direction. After a brief encounter with him, I concluded that the poor fellow may have had a few cells short of a full cortex. Consequently, I soon gave up the idea of meeting Mr. Perfect on campus and became involved in a multitude of activities instead. There was archery, ice hockey, swimming, skating, the Christian fellowship club, and the winter carnival.

Whenever I managed to spend a weekend at home, Mama made sure that I returned with a suitcase full of goodies, including homemade fudge (sucre à la crème) to share with my friends. That was her treatment for homesickness. No matter what little she had, Yvonne found a way to share it with others. It was part and parcel of who she was. As all mothers do, she occasionally shared some advice to help me negotiate the road of life. She once pointed out to me that in a world where right and wrong are often painted gray, " When you have a fight with your conscience and lose, you win." I tried to remember those words when facing hard choices in the years ahead. I also kept in mind Papa's teaching us the importance and power of the truth and how "falsehoods are termites in the trunk of a family tree." Such reminders were instrumental in keeping me on the straight and narrow, as I carried on with my studies.

The weeks on campus melted into semesters and these very quickly drifted by, and quite before I realized it had happened, I was writing my final exams and crossing the finish line. My college days were over and I was heading into the real world. Graduation was a proud moment for my family.

College

Papa's eyes twinkled so brightly that I was sure they cast a light into the crowd. With her limited means, Mama had managed to sew together an outfit to suit the occasion; and their presence seemed to bloom in the sea of faces on convocation day. At last one of their dreams had come true. They could not have radiated more pride if I had won an Olympic medal. With my diploma in hand, I was prepared to launch into my teaching career, and with the new income I planned to help my folks buy a house. I could hardly wait for September and my first classroom full of sun-ripened children. Looking back, I can only conclude that in all my achievements, my parents were my most loyal fans. They stood at every milestone as my inspiration, "the wind beneath my wings".

Macdonald College, 1959-1961.

My proud parents.

The Gathering of the Clan, 1960.

Mama came for a visit.

A New Career

It is better to light a candle
than to curse the darkness.

In due course, I was privileged to help my parents make a down payment on an old cottage. That dwelling with seven bedrooms would generate income with Mama's plan to open a boarding house. In 1962 Yvonne advertised lodging with meals for a reasonable rate. The idea soon caught on and, coinciding with the building of a hydroelectric project in the area, the business took off like a shot. Soon the house was a beehive of activity. Yvonne lavished all the energies of her generous nature upon the boarders. She rose at five every morning to light the wood stove and cook, scrub, launder, prepare box lunches and work non-stop into the night. Considering that she was now 58, this new venture would require extraordinary stamina. It seemed that her days never ended and when she finally dropped into bed at night she was totally exhausted.

For almost ten years, the "Pension" with down-home cooking on Gougeon Street was a coveted spot, very much in demand. When Papa was not working at odd jobs, he helped with the housework and laundry. There is an amusing anecdote related to this laundry duty. Mama had made a couple of batches of chokecherry wine, which she had stored in the basement. Whenever Leo did the laundry, she noticed that some wine went missing. One day when I came home from work, I overheard her calling down the trap door, "Leo, I can't hear you whistling." Papa came up with a big grin on his face and we both knew what he'd been up to, but in his own defense he claimed that the wine was medicinal. He sipped it as an "amendment to his constitution."

While she was running the "Room & Board" business, Mama bought bread in bulk quantities at reduced prices from a supermarket and then shared the loot at the same price with her neighbors. That way everyone enjoyed the benefits and there was no waste. That involved more work, but it was her way of helping the folks around her in a practical way. With the profits from their small business, they saved enough money to build their retirement home on the outskirts of town. Papa put in the labor and, together they achieved their goal, a cozy, two-bedroom bungalow in a lovely setting next door to Lizette's family. By the time they moved into their new home, we were all married and had children of our own, little ones who loved their visits with "Grandpapa and Grandmaman" in the country. Each was secure in the knowledge that he was loved unconditionally and sometimes, even spoiled just a little.

Though Mama did not like to talk about her physical condition, her health had suffered a setback at the "pension" where long days of relentless work had intensified her problems. By the time she retired at 68, Yvonne was suffering severe pain from arthritis in her hip. The reduced workload did not bring the relief she had anticipated, and she continued to suffer intense pain, which she bore with ferocious strength. Within five years, she would have to undergo total hip replacement surgery.

A New Career

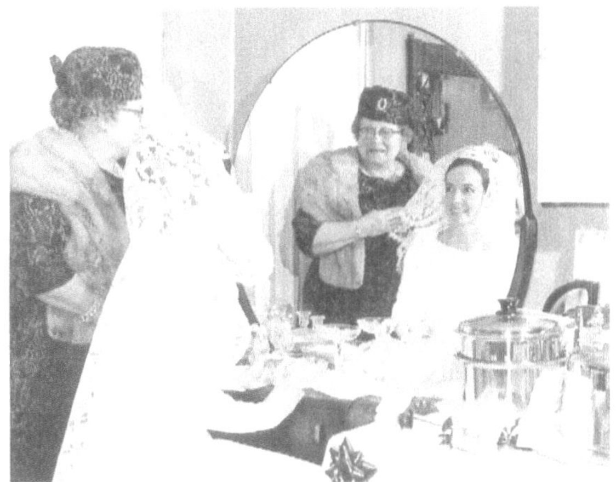

Mama at my wedding in Lachute,
October 1967.

Yvonne on her 60th birthday,
1964.

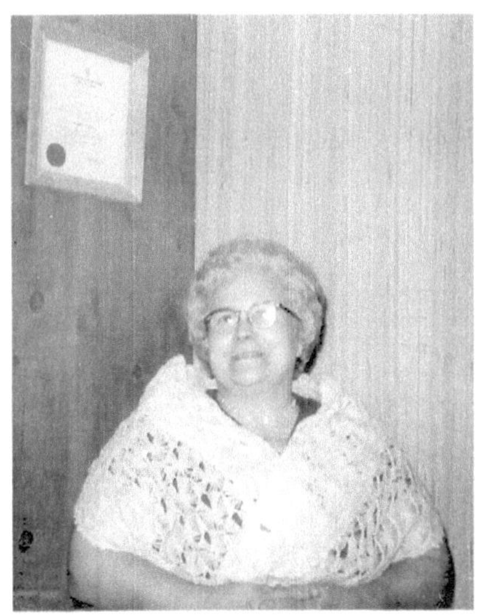

Yvonne in her new house.

Yvonne's family at their mother's 80th birthday. Annette, Hervé, Rose, Flore, Laurette, Domina, Grandmaman Petit, Yvonne, Antoinette, Armand, Irène in 1959.

A Last Farewell

Lives of great men all remind us
We can make our lives sublime
And departing, leave behind us
Footprints on the sands of time.
(Longfellow's "A Psalm of Life")

By the time Leo reached his sixth decade, his lungs were showing signs of distress. In spite of many attempts to quit the habit, Leo was unable to stop smoking. He had been smoking for over 50 years, a nicotine addict of the worst kind. At age 65 he was hospitalized for pneumonia from which he never completely recovered. That same autumn, the doctors diagnosed a malignant lung tumor, which did not respond to radiation treatments. Extremely weak and terribly thin, he asked to go home in mid-December. Together in their home, they dreamed of long ago. Hand in hand, they were walking back along the path of life with all its adversity. Through the haze that seemed to blanket the atmosphere, Mama recognized the inevitable. Our last visit with Papa was at home at Christmas. His face was ashen and the sparkle had gone from his eyes, like he had already seen death and was only waiting for it to strike. It was obvious that his soul and body were linked by the feeblest ties, and he was definitely moving toward eternity. We returned home with the memory of that image etched on our hearts, knowing that he would not recover. Mama's heart was torn by the added grief of being left alone in the home they had finally built for their retirement.

Two days after Christmas, we received the phone call. Papa was dead. What emptiness in those words! They were like the tomb itself. The shock over, the wound was laid bare. Yvonne was facing the deepest sorrow of her life and she let her grief express itself in sobs. A slave of grinding poverty for many years, it was another kind of slavery that finally claimed Leo's life, his addiction to nicotine. I personally experienced a significant reordering of my inner landscape. As I tried to cope with such a deep loss, I learned firsthand that tears are truly God's gift for the cleansing of the soul.

After the daze of the funeral in a blinding snowstorm, Yvonne was alone to face her tomorrows. Her life, it seemed, had been a series of goodbyes, but this one was so final. Oh, to be able to see the light behind the shadows that now crowded so thickly about her. As the weeks dragged by, the acute pain passed and only a dull ache remained, nothing in her heart but deadness. It took many months of grieving before time, the great healer, began to cover the wounds. In spite of his rough edges and quick temper, she had truly loved this man who had navigated life's turbulent waters by her side. As a team, they had lived through the shifting sunshine and shadow that make up a lifetime, as they crossed many dark valleys and shared impossible dreams. She now faced her twilight years alone in the house they had finally built together. A great emptiness lay ahead for her, a void that affected us deeply when we visited Mama. In an attempt to fill the gap, we spent weekends with her, but Papa's smiling face was no longer there to greet us from the front steps when we arrived and his absence was devastating.

The following summer, Yvonne had one more task to complete in order to bring closure to her grieving. Perhaps hungry for a hug from the past, she wanted to spend time alone on the old farm where she and Leo had started their married life together almost 40 years before. The very idea was a concern for the family, but she insisted and we respected her wishes. With the cottage well-stocked with food and water, we left her alone to mourn and reflect on the years she had spent in those surroundings. Without telephone or electricity, Yvonne had walked back into her past for a brief pause in the isolation that had shaped much of her life. All that remained was a chapter of memories and a closet full of heartaches. As she reflected on her life, she realized that the Lord had always been with her to bear the heavy end of the load. Her visits with former neighbors allowed her to express her feelings and perhaps release some pent-up regrets. When we returned for her, she was ready to let go and bury those hard years for good. The view of the house was blurred with tears as Yvonne cast a last look at the homestead. So much had happened here to shape our lives and endear so many memories to her heart, but that chapter was now closed.

One day when I was sitting with Mama, she began to chuckle. She wanted to tell me something but looked hesitant. About her eyes and mouth were the telltale wrinkles that told of a laughing heart. She still looked young and attractive. "Would you believe that a gentleman proposed to me?" It didn't sound ridiculous to me until she told me who it was, and we both roared with laughter. Yvonne had discarded her corsets but the stays were still tightly laced around her formidable Christian rectitude, and nothing could tempt her to so much as look at another man with romantic intentions. The incident had brought comic relief to her sober life.

From then on, Mama turned her mind and energies to new venues. God had built bigger plans into her heart and promises into her soul than she could imagine at that time. She devoted her time to helping anyone who crossed her path. At 69 she had many good years ahead to invest in creative projects, and she launched into a number of enterprising endeavors. Her first concern was for an adequate income. With only the government pension, she had to devise a way to make ends meet. With her usual resourcefulness, she proceeded to have her basement finished and built into an apartment, which she could rent. The resulting income would not only cover all the expenses of her house, but she could also benefit from the safety factor of not being alone. The end result was very successful and Mama remained an independent woman for many years. From the comfort of her house, she continued to touch many people with her generous spirit. Her living room became the chapel where a small group of Christian believers met for prayer and worship until they could afford a larger venue. It became obvious to those who cared to notice, that with the years, her poise and manner had gained in grace and compassion. She had the uncanny ability to see good things in unexpected places and talents in unexpected people, and God gave her the grace to tell them so.

People of all ages, even children and teenagers, loved to congregate in Mama's kitchen, where they were greeted by a bowl of firm, red-cheeked apples and a warm smile. Yvonne was a good listener, and one felt safe in her presence. She liked to say that she was not young enough to know everything or have all the answers. What folks witnessed when they met Mama was quite simply the essence of the godly woman that she was. Each shared his problems with someone who somehow understood. Perhaps it was because they did not feel threatened by this lady, who had suffered more than most in her lifetime and had plenty of love to pass around. She was a woman whose courage had been proven in the furnace of affliction and bent by the storms of adversity. Long ago King Solomon wrote in the book of Ecclesiastes 3:11 "God has made everything beautiful in its time." Those words enable us to trust Him to weave his loving purposes for us into the tapestry of time.

I once heard it said that, "Today, well lived makes every yesterday a dream of happiness and every tomorrow a vision of hope." It was during the autumn years of Yvonne's life that she became a refuge for many individuals seeking comfort. Mama took time to listen and pray for each one who stopped in. Family and neighbors alike called her "Grand-maman". Total strangers were touched by her generosity. Mama was persuaded that "one is never impoverished by giving"; on the contrary, she assured us that her life was enriched with every gift she was able to share, and these were numerous. One gift she did not hesitate to share was the gospel. Truth without love is dogma that does not touch the heart, she believed. Love without truth is sentimentalism that does not challenge the will. Truth must be spoken in love for God's spirit to reach the soul. Somehow Mama touched people's lives without apology, and folks did not resent it.

Several decades ago when I was growing up, 70 was retirement age when folks became eligible for old age security. Seventy was therefore associated with old age. That magic number crept up on Mama when she was living alone. We had planned a surprise party for her the Saturday following her seventieth birthday, so we phoned to inform her that we would be down on the weekend. The day she turned 70, her next-door neighbor found her sitting under a tree weeping. When asked what was the matter, Mama looked up through her tears sobbing, "Today is my birthday and I'm an old woman." Her friends tried to comfort her, but without apparent success. The day of her party, my husband's great-aunt Alida who was 90 at the time and very spry, smiled and assured her that 70 was still young. Mama smiled back with a sheepish grin. She understood that 70 was just a number, not a dead end on the road of life. There was plenty of living to do yet.

When Mama was living alone, my brother, Yvon, who lived in Saskatchewan, invited her to join his family on vacation. They traveled in his motor home across the Canadian Rockies and south across the border where they visited Yellowstone National Park, the Grand Canyon and many breathtaking sights along the way. It was the trip of a lifetime for Mama and Yvon's way of saying "Thank you, Mama. I love you." When she returned home, she was speechless. It had all been so grand, so extraordinary and beyond belief, a far cry from her humble background. We were thrilled and thankful that the Lord had granted such a blessing in her sunset years.

As she advanced in years, Yvonne was increasingly housebound. She confided in me that old age is not for sissies, "cause everything hurts, and what doesn't hurt won't move." With her usual sense of humor, Mama thought that she walked "with the grace of a hippo". She assured me that she was fine. It's just my body that's wilting; on the inside I can dance and sing." A new awareness of the fragility of life and the increasing pace of time drew our attention to her advancing years. Sometimes humor and tragedy can be such close kin. As time passed, her visits to the hospital increased in frequency and heightened our concern for her welfare. More than once she fell. She tried to explain how it happened but all she could recall was, "I was on my way to the bathroom when the floor just came up to greet me." And she had the bruises to show for it.

A Poem for Mama on her 80th Birthday

Aujourd'hui c'est un grand jour
Car nous fêtons vos cheveux blancs
Qui témoignent du long chemin
Qu'a parcouru notre grandmaman.

Vos rides qui tracent un beau sourire
Refètent le soleil levant.
Ce sont les jolies cicatrices
D'une vie remplie de durs moments

Sur une terre dans les montagnes,
Dans une cabane au fond du bois,
Sans eau courante ni téléphone,
Une lampe à l'huile, un poêle à bois.

Vous avez su vous débrouiller
Faire des conserves et jardiner,
Et assembler des couvre-pieds
Qui nous ont bien emmitouflés.
Traire les vaches, atteler les chevaux,
Râteler le foin au p'tit râteau,
Faire du beurre, pétrir du pain,
Elever des poules et faire du vin.

Madame Beausoleil prenait bien soin
De mesdames Torticolli et Bisancoin
Dans la cuisine ensoleillée
Les jours d'hiver d'un temps passé.

Le cœur brisé pour son Yvon,
Parti pour son éducation.
Vos larmes coulaient a l'abandon;
Quel sacrifice pour nos colons.

A Last Farewell

Dans ce grand fauteuil berçant
Avec un sourire rayonnant,
Entourée d'ceux qui vous aiment,
On vous adresse ce beau poème.

Grand-maman Yvonne at Lizette's house, Christmas 1988.

The End of a Long Journey

You may search my time-worn face;
You'll find a merry eye that twinkles.
I am not an old lady;
Just a little girl with wrinkles. (E. Bregnard)

When our dear mother was 82, she needed home care. None of us wanted to see her institutionalized where old people are parked along the walls like drooping houseplants in a daze. Lizette offered to take her in for a vacation until she felt well enough to return home. That visit extended indefinitely and Mama took up residence with their family. She occupied a room facing the kitchen on the main floor where she was never isolated from family activities. She was very conscious of their eventful schedules and remained as discreet as possible in her new quarters, never demanding and always so grateful for everyone's concern. Mama remained easy to live with to the end, recognizing perhaps that sour old people are the crowning works of the devil.

Though bound to the narrow perimeter of her bedroom by illness, "Grand-maman", as everyone called her, kept abreast of all the drama and was always present as an integral part of the family. In spite of her physical limitations, she was a strong spiritual force. Even in her twilight years, Mama looked at her children with pride. We were and always would be her trophies. The little ones inevitably nestled up to her lilac-scented plumpness. She was still warm and cuddly like a soft pillow with the same strong arms that wrapped around us like a safety belt; and still no other refuge felt more secure. She was beautiful, for even in this context, she seemed too alert to grow old and wrinkled. A certain dignity sat well on her as she listened quietly to each visitor.

Mama was on a special diet, but occasionally, with a wink, she tried to cheat when Lizette's back was turned. The children chuckled as they watched her reach for the "forbidden fare" and snatch a quick nibble. Those months brought a peaceful conclusion to her previously busy life. Family gatherings were happy times for young and old, further enriching our lives with a legacy of fond memories.

Mama's body was weak and unable to do her bidding. Her soul wanted to sympathize with it, and could have curled up and become bitter and ugly, but the Lord miraculously kept her spirit hopeful and positive through those long months. My sister, her youngest daughter, was a loving caregiver who nursed Mama with compassion and gentleness. As her illness progressed, Mama needed more help and we were all aware of what we stood to lose. Yet with every visit, I caught the fragrance of her love like a rose in bloom. It is a fact beyond any doubt that beautiful old people are works of art. Following a second stroke, heaven seemed nearer as Yvonne's now- painful journey toward eternity stretched on. Yet God was still walking with her, sheltering her in his love, and bottling up our tears in eternity. Even when life's journey led to illness and weakness, and she was confined to her bed, her years of fruitful service were not over. She could still pray. Prayer is one of the special privileges of infirmity, and in the end may be its greatest benefit. Above all else, she could love. Love remained her last and best gift to us. This was Mama's way of growing old with God.

We would not inherit a padded bank account or valuable jewels, but Mama would leave us her strength of character as a living legacy, her tremendous capacity to love and give of herself to all who crossed her path. Such was the impact that the gospel had on her life. She was not the kind of starry-eyed, trauma-inflicted individual who escapes from the realities of this world by incessantly talking about the golden streets of the world to come. Unlike those who feel that God's special blessings will fall first upon those who have favored Him by their occasional presence in church, Mama's faith was of a different brand. Though she firmly believed the promise of eternal life in heaven, Yvonne had both feet firmly planted in a practical faith, one that touched her fellow man. She once told me that one must not be so heavenly-minded as to be no earthly good.

In the beakers of honest analysis, how do I perceive the accomplishments of this little woman? Of course, I know that Yvonne was not perfect. A halo would have been just another thing to keep clean. Yvonne had very little tolerance for people who whined and complained. She was resourceful and expected no less from everyone else. She detested waste and in an attempt to be thrifty and find use for anything and everything, she became a packrat. Yvonne was a sensible person with many qualities, but that which distinguished her in my mind was her drive and motivation to deal creatively with every problem she faced. When life handed her a lemon, she made lemonade.

She had one great gift, which marked our lives from a very early age. It was her ability to build our self-esteem. We grew up convinced that we were the creator's masterpieces, the most attractive, most talented, and the most remarkable children on the face of the earth. I've discovered that people tend to fit the pattern and live up to the expectations set for them. It was a tall order for us to follow, but it had a positive effect on our lives as we attempted to please and "fill the bill". We did our best to justify her hopes and expectations. Whatever I have achieved in life, I am persuaded, is because I have stood on the shoulders of my parents. On the other hand, I grew up feeling that I must not fall short of perfection, and I was crushed by criticism or failure. It took years to outgrow that perception and accept myself with all my flaws and blunders. What has remained is the drive to "dare to try" to "go for it" and meet the challenge against all odds. Hence the writing of this book, which I would never have attempted without Mama's words echoing down through the years; "If other people can do it, so can you." And so, Mama, I've done it for you. I hope I've made you proud.

Back home from the hospital, her life was a fading page. Mama knew the end was near and had to reach through the fog that her soul's eye could not penetrate to find the "everlasting arm" on which to lean. As I walked in with a bouquet of flowers, an infinitely beautiful smile lighted the face which suffering had carved into arresting loveliness. She handled the blooms as if they were alive and breathing. I did not know at the time that it would be the last time we would talk and laugh together.

Death is the last chapter of time, but the first chapter of eternity; for as someone has said, "to live in hearts we leave behind is not to die". To her family, she had been like a teardrop on the cheek of time, like a jewel shining briefly. It was September 28, 1989 when I was called to the hospital. Mama had suffered a massive stroke. I spent the day by her side grieving as my mind traveled back over a lifetime of memories, the rich legacy of a very special woman. This time the lens of memory saw things I had left behind in my busyness. I remembered her peddling the old sewing machine by the window in our warm little kitchen, stitching clothes for her growing family, or assembling quilts for our beds. Then I could see her with a sprinkling bottle in one hand and a frilly organdy dress in the other, with the heavy iron heating on the stove. Then she was seated at Papa's old brown desk inking an argument as she wrote feverishly to the various levels of government in her unending struggle to improve the living conditions for our community, or thanking those who had contributed to her fundraising efforts for the church. Then my thoughts reverted to her standing perilously on top of the horse-drawn hay wagon holding the reins on the steep hillside, or butchering chickens in a cloud of feathers. Then she was stirring jam and humming a happy tune in the sunlit kitchen. I remembered her sad face as she had to deal with our prolonged absences and learned to trust the sanctuary of her home's protective walls in solitude. In another scene, she was efficiently serving 12 men seated around a long table. Then as the years added chapters to her life, I recalled the serene atmosphere in her house surrounded by friends and family. In every scene, I saw a strong woman who looked reality square in the face and met adversity head on.

"Not without design does God write the music of our lives" (John Ruskin). Looking back, I realize that Yvonne never accepted defeat, but fought the good fight with heart and soul. She taught her children by example that no matter how insignificant you might feel, you can make an impact. "If you think you are too small to make a difference," she insisted, "you've never been in bed with a mosquito." In a very few hours, the one everybody called Grand-maman would break the shackles of illness and old age, slipping from the bondage of her bed into the freedom of eternity. The loss of a mother is truly the first great sorrow that we grieve without her.

Yvonne was 85 when she left us, a very respectable age. With modern medicine, it is easy to live a long life in our society. Staying around a long time, however, should not be our primary goal. Rather we should give significance and value to all our years. How we finish the race depends largely on the pace we set along the way. Yvonne had been relentless in her pilgrimage and her funeral service rang with testimonies of her impact on so many lives. Judging from these, I believe that the following words had been at the heart of her focus:

"I expect to pass through this life but once. If I can show kindness to anyone or help someone, let me do it now as I will not pass this way again."

> Life was but a stopping place,
> A pause in what's to be,
> A resting place along the road
> To sweet eternity
> We all have different journeys,
> Different paths along the way.
> We all are meant to learn some things,
> But never meant to stay...
> Our destination is a place
> Far greater than we know;
> For some, the journey's quicker,
> For some, the journey's slow.
> When Yvonne's long journey ended,
> She left for her reward
> To find an everlasting peace,
> Together with her Lord.

Epilogue

What does man gain from all his labor
at which he toils under the sun?
Generations come and generations go,
but the earth remains forever. (Ecclesiastes 1:3)

*D*uring a recent visit to our abandoned homestead, I felt like a stranger from a distant past, treading on sacred ground. In spite of modern comforts, I found the area impoverished, because a vital part of the community is missing, its founding generation. Sadly, the narrow lanes that linked their homes have become busy roads and others are overgrown with brush. I could almost hear the wind carry the familiar words of greeting, "How are you?"

"Oh, juss tolerable. Got a ketch in me back. Muss be de rumatis agin."

The 20 acres of fields had reverted to forest. Three of the original buildings were gone, torn down by thieves who found uses for the lumber. One generation is all it takes to erase a lifetime of labor. Behind the tall trees stand the stern-faced cliffs clothed in green moss. The little dam was washed out in a spring flood, leaving the pond almost empty. Daylilies were shouldering their way up through the tall foliage by the old well.

As we ambled down the lonely hill, the sun dropped behind the ridge firing a crimson sky. The noises, smells and voices of long ago filled my mind. Why was I speaking in hushed tones usually reserved for churches and funerals? Perhaps the memories were sacred. I could almost see the trees smiling at the memory of my fledgling attempts at downhill skiing in that very spot when the path had been choked with snow in the wake of a storm. The barn was gone, but on the ancient concrete floor, I recognized the old Hudson engine, lying upside down like a corpse. The tiny seedling I had planted the year we moved is now a majestic tree with limbs reaching across the yard to the house. There was an ache in my chest as we approached the old cottage.

The drawn shades and smokeless chimney gave the house a stricken look, as if carrying the weight of a great sorrow. When we entered the house, the sun had crawled into bed and dusk was stealing over the land. I thought that a little fire in the stove might warm its old bones. I lit the lantern against the gathering darkness and it cast ghostly shadows on the walls. A flicker of memory pushed the years back to the days of long ago. My heart skipped, then made up for the lost beat in double time. I could not suppress a shiver. I had just traveled back 40 years and stepped into my childhood. Anyone returning to a childhood home is surprised to find how small it is. I could remember when the tabletop was about eye level and I shared the floor under the table with a black kitten. Our house seemed much bigger then. I had stepped back into the once-crowded world of our little kitchen, but the voices were silent. Vandals had come and trundled away most of the belongings. I felt violated by the damage, but I was thankful that Mama had been spared the sight. She would have died a little inside, because this had been her home for so many years, a warm cave-place for her family by the wood stove, on the homestead where it all began so many years ago.

Why did I bother to write this story? Perhaps when we are nothing but dust and teeth and bones, this record may be all that is left of our brief passing on this earth.

Grand-maman Yvonne did not live to meet her 15 great-grandchildren, but I trust that through this book, they will wish they had known her, and be inspired by the person she was.

Epilogue

22-year old Leola
teaching in Lachute.

School photo of ten-year-old
Leola in Namur.

Leola at 50
in St-Lazare.

Acknowledgements

I wish to thank my husband for his patience as he taught me how to use the computer when I first began to write this book in 2002. He also showed me how to scan and insert photos into the text and came to my rescue every time I ran into trouble and feared that I might have lost my entire book.

My manuscript had been sitting in a drawer for some 12 years when my friend, Sheila Hébert, suggested I consult Louise Sproule, editor of The Review in Vankleek Hill. Thank you, Sheila, for your input. Ms Sproule very quickly put me at ease and helped me through the steps to the publishing of this volume with so much professionalism and knowledge. I greatly appreciate all your work, Louise, and would recommend your services to anyone looking for advice and direction to publish their writing.